SO CAL

Dispatches from the End of the World

Joe Donnelly

Punk ★ Hostage ★ Press

SO CAL
Dispatches from the End of the World
Copyright © Joe Donnelly 2022
An imprint of Punk Hostage Press
ISBN: 978-1-940213-18-7

Cover Art
The L.A. Collection #5 and #6
by Elisa Saether and Ingrid Allen.

Punk Hostage Press
Hollywood, USA
punkhostagepress.com

For Ingrid

FOREWORD

"Your work is your memoir," a writer friend once told me over a plate of huevos rancheros at Café Zinque in Venice. She was referring specifically to nonfiction — journalism, profiles, essays, travel pieces, etc. The idea is that once we writers amass a substantial body of work, the topics and subjects we chose to immerse ourselves in become us. They are the show in the "show, don't tell" maxim.

Such is the case with *So Cal: Dispatches from the End of the World*, Joe Donnelly's second collection of nonfiction. The title says a lot. The bulk of the pieces are set in the lower third of the Golden State, and even when they're not they ooze a certain SoCal leaning. The characters are varied. Jim Evans is an artist/art director who designed album covers for Neil Young, the Beach Boys, Beastie Boys and Beck. Danny Kwock is a surf star turned surf-wear mogul. James Goldstein is a fashionista/basketball lover/mystery man who lives in a John Lautner–designed home that features in that SoCal-est of movies, *The Big Lebowski*. Max is a scarred-up German shepherd who reminds Joe to smell the roses, poppies and sunflowers.

Then, there is the road. In "The Tortoise and the Tank," Joe and the artist/Dogtown documentarian C.R. Stecyk head out to the Mojave Desert in search of endangered tortoises (or, more specifically, endangered tortoises being relocated per the Defense Department). Joe's chronicling of their odyssey takes on a cinematic glint — and will forever imbue my (and maybe your) future desert trips. In "The Loneliest Road in America," Joe thinks "unoriginal thoughts about life and what it had and hadn't turned out to be." His soon-to-be ex-girlfriend has given Joe's bed to her new lover, and rubber-on-bitumen and skin-on-sheets do parallel play.

Who is Joe? I posed this question to the writer Arty Nelson. He and Joe met at Jefferson Elementary in Pittsburgh. Joe is godfather to one of Arty's sons. "Joe has a real gift for making the personal universal," said Arty. "He's always been civically engaged. For the people, by the people — that's a strong gear in his machine."

Who is Joe? I asked C.R. Stecyk. Along with their desert trip, C.R. and Joe have worked together on a bunch of stories. "Joe is a man with no limits on how far he will go, both in terms of the pursuit of a story and in the conjuring up a unique way of telling it."

Who is Joe? I asked myself.

We met in the mid-'90s when he was editor of *Stick*, a snowboard magazine. Curious. Erudite. Intellectual. But don't cross him. Half a decade later, he was an editor at *New Times Los Angeles* and then the *LA Weekly*. I was impressed by his catholic interests and his prolific journalism (he wrote an indelible profile of Sean Penn). Disillusioned by the bottom-line interests of the new publisher, and alarmed by the trends in algorithm-driven media, Joe and *LA Weekly* co-editor Laurie Ochoa founded *Slake*, a slow-cooked, long-form, almost anti-digital literary journal. In a "getting the band back together" moment, a group of inveterate L.A. writers were reunited. Readings and parties and dinners — and some excellent SoCal-centric work — ensued.

The thing about Joe is he's so busy championing his friends, it's easy to forget what a great writer he is. Reading through the pieces that follow, I was floored by his ability to breathe freshness into every scene and description. Sometimes the more work the artist produces, the more the tropes/defaults/repetitions become glaring. Not the case here.

Who is Joe? Read ahead, and you'll get a good picture.

~ Jamie Brisick, former pro surfer and author of Becoming Westerly: Surf Legend Peter Drouyn's Transformation into Westerly Windina and We Approach Our Martinis with Such High Expectations

CONTENTS

PART ONE

I Know You, Rider

"The future is wide open, and it's going
to start as soon as I make that exit."

CONTEMPLATING CASSADY

Originally published in Huck Magazine

Woe be to ye who follow the way of the Holy Goof, for your reward, well, it isn't likely to be earthly — at least not as it's been sold. And for it to be something else, you're going to have to believe in something else. And if you don't, you're just going to have to believe that living like the Holy Goof is the right way to live; that your reward will be life itself.

Kerouac's personification of Neal Cassady, aka Dean Moriarty, as his Holy Goof refers back to the apostle Paul who tells the Corinthians that he and his crew are fools for Christ, a ragged band, despised, "made as the filth of the world." In other words, they're beat. Their poverty and their lack of interest in the trappings of polite society has made them pure.

As Dean Moriarty said to Sal Paradise — or as Cassady said to Kerouac — "Everything is fine, God exists, we know time. Everything since the Greeks has been predicated wrong. You can't make it with geometry and geometrical systems of thinking. It's all this!"

Sal, though, is in limbo. Somewhere between Paul and the Corinthians. Somewhere between Dean and dreams of a house with a white picket fence. Somewhere between Whitman's wild, pure America and the America of Sloan Wilson's *The Man in the Gray Flannel Suit*, which would come out just a year before Jack Kerouac's *On the Road*.

Dean's life — his glory and his folly — puts the question right to Sal, just as Neal Cassady likely did to Kerouac. How d'you want to live, son? Is it this, or is it that? Are you you? Or are you who it/they/the system wants you to be?

This is a question American men have been struggling with since the frontier closed and the farms became mechanized and cities, suburbs and exurbs became the country's organizing principles. Wilson's book suggests you can be both; that you can maintain some internal integrity while selling out on the surface. Some call it adulthood. But I'm not sure. It's a rift I have yet to settle within myself, despite having been around for nearly half a century, almost as long as the Holy Goof, Moriarty, has been *On the Road*.

I know you, rider.

I moved eight times by the time I was ten: out of state, out of country, back in country, south, north, bottom to middle to top. By the time I was 31, I had moved 17 times. West, further west, north, south, east, west again, west again.

***

This peripatetic existence might have worn out Kerouac himself, and looking back it was most definitely the same quest for self-knowledge and God-knowledge that inspired Dean and Sal's adventures, but it was also the result of schizophrenic vacillation between the two sides of myself I couldn't, like the hero of *The Man in the Gray Flannel Suit*, reconcile. I yearned for comfort, for a home and a hearth somewhere away from the chaos I came from, but I also put the possibility in my rearview mirror every time it finally seemed within my grasp. Some Cassady in my ear always seemed to shake me up and send me on my way just when I was getting somewhere. The real me, he said, was out there somewhere. I just hadn't found him yet.

College was my first stab at convention. I went to a pricey school that specialized in turning out future masters of the universe who consistently voted Republican and worshipped America without, it seemed, knowing it very well.

Which could explain why I gravitated to the great Drozini. Drozini was a couple years older than I. In a school populated with preps, he dressed in tattered flannels and jeans. His hair was never combed and hardly ever washed. He wore a long, black wool overcoat that shrouded him in mystery. He was a superstar high-school athlete who blew out a knee and then smoked excessively. He had an unmatched stamina for drink and drugs. He spoke in parables ("Take two or it's not worth it") and refused to give a shit about the relentless strivings going on all around us. Like Jack, his father was dead and I knew, somehow, that this was the center of his sadness.

I'd drive with him in the sullen, snow-dusted valleys of Chenango County and down into green Pennsylvania, through Maryland, and into all of the nameless mid-Atlantic. Like Cassady, he was a moocher and a con. The poorest guy at our rich school, perhaps. A user. I'd drop him off at his mother's house. She'd feed us and show pictures of Drozini from high school when he ruled the known world. The hallways of that house were haunted in black and white and the world outside was getting less known all the time.

Drozini changed my course. Or confirmed it. I'm not sure. Like Kerouac, he was a master at showing and not telling, leaving his audience to its own imagination.

As I was at school on athletic grants, I quit the jock life and started reading novels and history books. Philosophy. Grew more curious about the world west of the Hudson River than most of my now very successful friends. I kept moving, shuffling, searching for me and God and reinventing myself along the way. I shook my fist at the sky a lot.

In the process I became a dilettante of the American margins, seeking subcultures and trying them on for size. I'd excavate for artifacts of Lou Reed's Lower East Side. When that ran its course, I'd go to the mountains and cop the persona of Craig Kelly, fashion myself a soul rider in harmony with the elements, no parks or pipes, only the mountain. In the West Coast cities, I'd study the legends of Miki Dora and Jay Adams, cop their personas, hitch their rides. In the bars I was Bukowski, brawling and breaking noses, mostly my own.

Who were these American archetypes and who was I among them? What is the content of our character more than 50 years after *On the Road* posed the question? Are we holy fools or are we company men? Do we go bop or go bang? And, as Carlo Marx said to Sal and Dean, "I mean, man, whither goest thou? Whither goest thou, America, in thy shiny car in the night?" And to which Dean answered back, "Whither goest thou?"

Yes, whither, indeed.

THE LONELIEST ROAD IN AMERICA

Originally published in the LA Weekly

Route 50 is a capricious, two-lane highway running through the middle of Nevada and western Utah like a sclerotic artery. It has the audacity to call itself the Loneliest Road in America.

Nevada, at least, has a sense of humor about Route 50 (does Utah have a sense of humor about anything?). When you gas up at either end of the state, they give you a survival map and a passport to stamp at each of the towns separated by long empty stretches along the way. West to east it goes: Carson City, Fallon, Austin, Eureka, Ely. If you make it to the end you get a certificate saying, "Congratulations! You Survived the Loneliest Road in America." I've survived the trip many times. In fact, I've more than survived it. At various points in my life, I've embraced it, scoffed at it and challenged it to hit me with its best shot.

The first time, a willful act of separation led me there. You know the drill — heiress girlfriend decides to get serious about life, goes off to business school, marries and leaves you to your own devices in the big city. Once the doctors recommended a change in lifestyle, I beat a retreat for Vail, Colorado, to become a ski bum and find myself. I found Route 50.

It was the spring of '91, after my first winter in Vail when the ski season had melted to a halt. Work gets hard to find during the off-season, and cash becomes scarce. Folks start drinking too much and hitting each other too often. Running out of money myself, I sold the '85 Jeep I'd arrived in and bought a '78 Subaru wagon. Subarus don't win many style points, but this one, tan with a deer guard in front, had a mutt-like charm and was just as game. I liked to imagine that if everything fell off that car except the steering wheel, I'd only have to hold on and it would drag me forward.

With the cash left over from trading the Jeep, I decided to road-trip out to San Francisco and swing down the coast. If you're heading to the Bay Area, conventional wisdom says take Interstate 70 to the middle of Utah and then jog north on I-15 to I-80. That way you never go more than 50 miles without gas, food or lodging. Looking at the map, though, Route 50 seemed the straighter shot. I saw that for most of the way only two towns, Ely and Fallon, were marked in bold, and there was a long way between them. I noticed also that Ely and Fallon were in smaller lettering than, say, Carson City or Sparks, but from the looks of the map, they were bustling metropolises compared to Eureka or Austin, which were noted in the tiniest and thinnest lettering. No matter. I was a loner-seeker, and my mysterious aura would be enough to keep highway robbers, lobos and loons at a safe distance.

When you're not exactly screaming down the road at 65 mph (the wagon's top speed), the great basins of south-central Utah stretch out like an endless *Road Runner* storyboard. It's beautiful country, but it feels rigid and formal, lacking in human impulse. Entering into the burnt, red terrain of Nevada, though, my heart rose. It was just as vast and empty as Utah, but for some reason seemed more inviting, like a giant hearth. The time between oncoming cars increased to the degree that I thought I might really be the only traveler out there, but it wasn't a scary emptiness that confronted me. It was nourishing. I drove my Subaru hard through the desert, rising and ascending plateaus and plains, desert brush clinging to shady pockets in the mountain passes. I drove and drove, thinking unoriginal thoughts about life and what it had and hadn't turned out to be. I was aware that family and friends wondered what was wrong with me — leaving behind New York, career opportunities, relationships and other things I wasn't ready for, becoming hard to track down, disappearing into the West, setting off on uncharted courses . . . Sometimes I wondered, too.

In the middle of nowhere, with one hundred miles to the next stop, the Subaru overheated. I pulled over to the side, got out my guitar, lit a cigarette and played a few cowboy songs just to let the desert know I came in peace. Something happened out there in the dusk on that road with the sun setting down on foreign lands and everything turning purple. I could smell poppies in west China. I could taste fruits from the South Seas. I could sense time moving like a faraway swell in the ocean: It was out there, but I wasn't yet caught in its wave. I realized everyone I knew before was already a memory and that this wasn't just a phase. My life was somewhere out here. After a while, I put some coolant in the engine and pressed on.

Another time on another trip, I drove a different, even older Subaru (downward mobility was my mode back then) through the desert with the temperature hovering around 110. When I made it to Fallon, an Air Force town, I was caked with dust and slightly disoriented from the heat. I pulled into a KFC, ordered a bucket of chicken and fries, poured a large water over my head and drove on to San Francisco where I ran into (literally) the only Swedish model at the party. Turns out we had a lot in common: I spoke English and she was a Swedish model. A cab driver taken with the romance of it all drove us around the city, picking up fares and advisers along the way, until he found us a vacant love nest in the fully booked city. The morning revealed it to be a Tenderloin flophouse.

A snowboarder friend joined me on another trip to the coast. We started drinking as soon as we crossed into Utah, tossing 40-ouncers into the back of my pickup truck like they were candy wrappers. Somewhere in Utah, we picked up an eccentric older guy we called Uncle Bob. Uncle Bob was on his way to an algae convention in Eugene, Oregon. He showed us his briefcase full of rare specimens that he claimed had magical health benefits. He ran down his get-rich-quick scheme and tried to get us to invest. The three of us drank and laughed our way across Route 50, stopping for steak and eggs and petty larceny whenever the occasion arose. Once I drove straight from San Francisco to Denver via Route 50 — 20 hours if it was a minute — popping caffeine pills and drinking Coke the whole way just to get back to a girl who wasn't expecting me.

I had gone native.

The point is, Route 50 is always an option, never a necessity, like betting on an iffy hand. When you're young you tend to push your luck just for kicks. But the house always wins in the end. Some learn the hard way. Some just take a wrong turn at the wrong time.

***

The only thing that's changed in Eureka, Nevada, since its Wild West heyday is the internal-combustion engine, running water, electricity and the male-to-female ratio, which has gotten worse over the years as the mines shut down and the old Opera House and bordello turned into a motel with slot machines in the lobby. A sign at the town limits says: *Welcome to the Loneliest Town on the Loneliest Road in America.*

It had been a couple of years since those first carefree jaunts through the desert had taken me through Eureka. Going back to school had finally propelled me out of Vail and the low-end jobs and seasonal-affective disorders that were leading to too many broken bones and misdemeanors. Near the end, I cashed in my last Subaru and was down to a Honda Hawk motorcycle and a lot of mud in my teeth. The last straw came when a skid/loader on a construction site conked out on the crest of a hill and nearly toppled me into a swimming pool. The tip of my ring finger was almost chopped off in the hydraulic arm. I got out, washed off my hand, inspected my mangled finger and started kicking the mini-tractor, yelling, "Fuck this fucking place. I'm out of here!" over and over again until someone took me to the hospital.

By and large the years in journalism school and working at various newspapers were good years, culminating in a plum assignment to *The Washington Post*. But all good things come to an end, and this one ended suddenly. Before I knew it, I'd quit the *Post* and was traveling back across the country to pick up my stuff at the place in Los Angeles I used to share with a woman who used to be my girlfriend but, while I was in D.C., had taken up with a Viking from Iceland.

I knew I wouldn't be able to do this errand without some help, so I called my old friend Arty. I could barely form a sentence. He could tell this was serious and flew out to meet me in New York. From there we set out for L.A. where I'd leave Arty and then retreat once again to the sanctuary of Vail. The recidivism of it all left me nearly comatose. The entire drive went by in a blur of cigarettes, cupcakes and Nine Inch Nails CDs. It was November and the gray sky was as heavy as the music and my mind.

"Arty, she gave him the bed," I said somewhere around St. Louis, grabbing a Ho Ho from my box of 24. It might have been the first thing I said the entire trip.

"What?"

"She gave the Viking our bed. I mean *my* bed. She gave it to him." It wasn't just a bed. It was the first bed I had ever bought. The first time I ever had a bed that was my own. It was a symbol of having made my way up off the floor. Now it was in the loft next door. I asked her how she could be so heartless.

"I didn't think you'd mind," she said. "You weren't going to use it, and he needed a bed." She made it sound like I was being immature.

"Dude, that's cold," Arty said in the car, polishing off a limited-edition Hostess Snowball eight-pack.

"What am I going to do? I mean, how could she be that insensitive?"

"I don't know, dog, that's a tough one." He was eyeing the Dolly Madisons.

"I'll be damned if I'm going to have Vlad the Impaler fucking her on it."

Arty shook his head sympathetically and reached for one of my Ho Hos. "Hey, have you heard the new Cypress Hill CD?"

By the time we reached Colorado, we were both weighed down with junk food and soda, but there was nothing to do about it but press ahead. The next stretch in L.A. would be the tough one — I didn't need to deal with Route 50 just yet. We took the safe route, I-70 to I-15 South.

***

I hadn't seen her in about six months. I thought about the ring inscribed with the words *forget me not* that she had given me when I left for the *Post* gig. Back in D.C., I would go to the mailbox every day looking for something that explained it all. Instead I got forwarded bills. I fingered the ring in my pocket: *Forget me not.* Fat chance.

My father's Buick LeSabre was impressive as we headed toward Las Vegas. It had an understated luxuriousness. Ninety felt the same as 55. The steering was responsive. The miles flew by in silence, save for the crinkle of individually wrapped Dolly Madisons. Arty was playing every CD in the Soul Assassins catalog. I think we were up to Funkdoobiest. We were getting closer and fatter.

"Arty, what am I going to do about the bed? I mean, I can't take it with me." We were at the Coco's in Barstow, eating chocolate cake.

"Look, man, if it's bothering you that much, you gotta do something about it. You gotta call her."

I told her I wanted the bed out of there.

"What do you want me to do with it?" she asked, like there was no other option.

"I want you to call Salvation Army and have them pick it up."

"What?"

"You heard me. That bed better be fucking out of there when I come to pick up my shit."

"I don't get it."

"I know you don't, but you should."

***

I dropped Arty off in Hollywood and made my way to the loft she and I rented at the Brewery. It was empty when we moved in. I put in the cabinets. Unfortunately, I put them in upside down and the doors opened the wrong way — my own forget-me-not.

It was cold and overcast when I arrived. She was waiting outside, wearing that sweater, the one that made her look like Marilyn Monroe. I wanted to be angry when I saw her, but I was just sad and felt like a fool. That sweater was like six daggers in my heart. I picked up my belongings. The bed was propped up on display in the hallway. It was just an appeasement. I knew Thor would be using his hammer on it before I was out of the county. I had to let it go.

If there ever was a sadder-looking sap than I was in the parking lot, loading my shit into the car, staring at her in that sweater, my feet cinder blocks, I would have liked to have met him. She gave me a hug goodbye. I wanted to refuse it, but I couldn't. I handed her back the ring. "You may need this," I said, and drove away.

It started raining while I was on the 101 North, heading up to Oakland to see my uncle. I pulled over and called her. I didn't have anything to say. I just cried.

"You gotta stop this," she said, not unkindly. "It's gonna be okay. You're a great guy. You deserve better than me anyway."

I didn't want better, not then. I wanted my pride back. I wanted to know why she didn't want me. I wanted to know why, despite my best efforts, despite J school, the front-page stories and the breakfasts with editors who told me how great I was, I was still heading back to the place I had tried so hard to get away from. Driving back to Vail, I meant to take Interstate 80. I knew I was in no condition to meet up with my old traveling companion, the Loneliest Road in America. Somehow, though, with my head a mush of regret, I missed the turnoff at Sacramento, and I-80 turned into Route 50 all on its own. I didn't even notice until I was past south Lake Tahoe and out in the wilds. It started raining as soon as it was too late to turn back. I should have stayed in Fallon, but there were too many miles to go and, besides, it was just rain.

By the time I was approaching Austin, where the shoulders drop off the road as it winds through the mountains, the rain had turned to snow. By the time I was past Austin, with 70-some miles to make Eureka, the snow had turned to a blizzard. Visibility was about 10 feet. I slowed to a crawl and put on my hazards. If I stopped, a truck would come up behind and crush me, but there was almost no way to go on. One wrong move would send me tumbling down a hillside where I would have to wait days or weeks for someone to find my charred body. I should have kept the ring, I thought. How poetic if the ring was the only thing left to identify me.

I felt like God was testing me, and I wasn't in the mood for it. Gripping the steering wheel so tightly my knuckles went from white to blue, I started yelling back. *Fuck you! Fuck you! You're not going to kill me you motherfucker!* I thought about the fancy dinner thrown by the managing editor of the *Post* and how someone kicked over the beer bottle I'd set on the floor, the liquid slowly spreading like a plague toward the fancy rug that probably cost more than I'd made in the last two years. I thought about how maybe I shouldn't have knocked over that one intern to catch the ball in the outfield at the staff-versus-editors softball game — but he would have missed! Maybe I shouldn't have hit the home run that won the game the staffers are supposed to lose each year. Maybe I shouldn't have played footsie under the bar with that impish editorial assistant when we all went out for drinks. Maybe I shouldn't have been making out with her in the hallways. Maybe I shouldn't have gotten drunk before writing that one story — even if it ended up the section lead. Maybe I should have been more humble and kissed more ass. Maybe I should have said yes when they told me they couldn't give me a staff job, but wanted me to stay on for another two-month contract. Instead I told them to fuck off and took a job and a ski pass from the paper in Vail. What was I proving to whom?

Maybe I should have paid more attention to my ex-girlfriend when I had the chance.

I was guilty, all right. I was guilty of a lot of things. Things I couldn't even remember. After all, I was a white male, the guiltiest. But all I could think was *fuck you all anyway*. My father's LeSabre, an unlikely hero if ever there was one, held the road. I was vibrating with stress by the time I passed the sign welcoming me to Eureka: the Loneliest Town on the Loneliest Road in America. I pulled into the old bordello and inquired about a room. Everything stopped. You could have heard a thousand pins drop one at a time. I looked around and noticed I was the only one without a trucker's cap and a ZZ Top beard. All eyes were on me. To them, I was either an alien or the prettiest thing that had stopped in there in years.

***

The rooms were upstairs, off a balcony, just like the Old West. Everybody watched me climb the stairs and unlock the door. I had to laugh at the waterbed in my room. *Great, at least when I'm gang-raped by a bunch of out-of-work miners, it'll be on a waterbed.* I sat in the room for an eternity, shivering. What am I going to do? I couldn't just sit there. Fuck it, I decided. If I'm going to go down, I'm going to go down the best way I know how.

I went downstairs to the bar and ordered a shot of whiskey and a beer. Then I ordered another. Then I put my quarters on the pool table. I ended up playing a wiry miner with half a set of teeth who told me everyone was stuck there until the mine reopened. I knew the feeling. I asked him what they did for kicks. He said they drank, took speed and stockpiled weapons, "in case the n—s decide they want to come up from Las Vegas." I nodded my head and slipped one of the five-inch construction nails sitting on a dusty ledge into my pocket. I flashed back to a story I had read in the *Deseret News* years before about a rash of unsolved murders in the area. We played a couple games of eight ball. I fantasized about sticking the nail in that asshole's throat, but I bought him a beer instead.

When I finally was drunk enough not to care what happened next, I went up to my room and propped a chair under the door handle — I mean, they were at least going to rob me. I put the nail on the nightstand. I sunk into the waterbed and thought about that swell of time off there in the distance. It had caught me at last, and it was a tidal wave.

Congratulations, I said to myself, you're the Loneliest Man in the Loneliest Town on the Loneliest Road in America.

The next morning, the sun was brilliant and the air crystalline. The desert appeared refreshed by the snow. Route 50 invited me back onto it like it was a friend from long ago. Before I got in the LeSabre, I looked up, shook my fist, and drove on.

MESSIAH WOLF

Originally published in Zyzzyva

When I was a boy, my imagination was ripe for wolves. But, it wasn't the usual folktales and fables that got to me, or the scenes of wolf packs airbrushed onto the panel vans of my suburban youth. At six years old, my wolf was a companion, not a cautionary tale or a signifier of being born to be wild. As far as I can recall, some of my first (and last) unencumbered moments were spent on the porch of our South New Jersey home on rainy summer afternoons, watching big drops chase little drops down the screen while *Peter and the Wolf* played in the background and those French horns signaled the arrival of something as wild and doomed as any six-year-old boy. There, I daydreamed of adventures to be had and redemptions to be won by my wolf and me.

Of course, my wolf sidekick was a construct. One formed of the reams of mostly fanciful received knowledge about wolves our psyches start getting fed at an early age, accelerated in my case, no doubt, by the suggestiveness of my German shepherd and the trick of music on my child's brain. What creature other than wolves has been such a big part of our lives and such a small part of our experiences?

That I would daydream in some abstract idea of *wolf* is not all that surprising. The abstract is where Americans have been most comfortable with wolves ever since we brutally purged them, along with Native Americans, from most of our lands. In the abstract, they are usefully totemic. In the abstract, we can call on them when we want to summon a little nostalgia for the primal past or a bit of remorse for burying it in mass graves. There, they don't demand too much of us, nothing that requires any sacrifice.

More recently, though, wolves have been gaining ground on terra firma. Once relegated to bands of holdouts in Northern Michigan, Minnesota and Wisconsin, the number of gray wolves in the lower 48 states has more than doubled to about 6,000 following their mid-'90s reintroduction to the Rocky Mountain West. They are getting closer all the time. At least seven now live in Northern California after being absent for nearly a century.

The current wolf population is still just a tiny fraction of its historical numbers distributed across a tiny fraction of its historical habitat. Even so, the growing presence of wolves in a landscape that is much messier than a six-year-old boy's imagination is forcing a long-overdue reckoning that, like so many others, we might still not be ready for.

Nobody said salvation was going to be easy.

***

It certainly doesn't seem so when I find myself waking up dry-mouthed and dizzy next to a woman in a room in a fancy hotel neither of us could afford.

It's the winter of 1989 and I am two decades and thousands of miles from Prokofiev and that screened-in porch in South Jersey, on a ski trip in Lake Louise, Alberta, Canada. In a few years, a lanky Iowan by the name of Carter Niemeyer will venture into the frozen tundra north of here, trap a few dozen wolves and bring them back to the remote mountain wildernesses of Wyoming and Idaho where they will quickly set the aforementioned reckoning in motion.

I've been wandering around a different kind of wilderness, that of an unmoored early adulthood lacking any sense of direction or purpose. I'm on this ski trip with a bunch of fathers and sons from Pittsburgh, the city where my family eventually settled. Pittsburgh isn't known for skiing because the skiing in Pittsburgh sucks. But the *going skiing* signifies.

See, by 1989, the last of the big steel mills had shuttered and the city's nosedive from third-largest corporate headquarters in the U.S. to one of its suicide capitals was complete. Even the once-eternal Steelers dynasty had been gathering dust for nearly a decade. For these fathers and sons of Pittsburgh, this ski trip to Lake Louise, Alberta, signals they've made it through the initial wave of Rust Belt regression with some of their bourgeois aspirations intact. They are here to celebrate that.

They are also mostly too young for their marriages and their children and the conventional lives they've struggled to attain. So, when the celebration moves to the fancy hotel's disco bar — picture a well-appointed Holiday Inn lounge from a Boston suburb somehow transplanted into the bowels of a gorgeous Victorian chateau in the middle of the Canadian Rockies — they take an overbearing interest in my flirtations with a cocktail waitress. Right around last call, the men pass a hat, literally, to get us a room.

In the morning, I stumble outside for a scheduled group photo, leaving the girl dreaming in a high thread count. The men greet me with cheers and slaps on the back. Still woozy, I take a gulp of cold, clean air and wonder if thrills are always going to be this cheap. The air, though, is something else. It tastes ancient and unspoiled at the same time, a brand-new sensation. I take another gulp and smile for the photo op, the snow-covered Canadian Rockies in the background.

Next, we board a bus for a tour of the glaciers around Banff National Park. I sit by myself, doing my best to take in the scenery while pondering my hangover and run-of-the-mill malaise. The men don't seem to be similarly burdened. They are drinking and growing restless. After looking at a couple of glaciers, they demand the bus return to the hotel — the disco bar calls. Someone says, "You've seen one giant hunk of blue ice, you've seen them all," and everyone laughs.

Those were the days.

On the way back to the hotel, the bus crosses a low bridge over a train track that runs through a narrow valley separating two peaks. An easement girds each side of the tracks before it's overtaken by tree and slope. The bus moves slowly across the bridge — maybe there is ice. As it creeps along, I stare out the window, pondering how the tracks look like a lazy creek. Then, something catches my eye: a large, dark figure about 50 yards away, sauntering alongside the tracks.

I watch it move. It seems so at home, so devoid of neuroses . . . so unlike us. I'm mesmerized. When it stops for a moment to look back toward the bus, a jolt of recognition, maybe even connection, shoots through me. I must have said it in my head a few times before the words make it out of my mouth. "Wolf, wolf, *WOLF!*"

My fellow travelers are unmoved. I point out the window and say it again: "Wolf!"

But, it's gone.

The guy who'd had enough of looking at glaciers says it was probably just a coyote and everyone agrees and that's that. Who could blame them, what did we know of wolves then, other than as cartoons characters and team mascots?

I can't summon the faces from that trip, but I can still see those blazing, imperious eyes looking through me with something innate and fierce. My first encounter with a real wolf was more than I'd ever imagined as a boy.

I like to think that wolf could have been OR-7's great, great, great, great grandfather.

***

More than 20 years later, summer is turning to fall and no one yet
knows of OR-7 when a woman and her husband set out from
McCall, Idaho, on motorcycles. They are going to visit relatives
in Weaverville, California, just west of Redding. It's a long ride,
traversing more than 600 miles and a time zone.

They probably start out on Route 95 South, which shadows
the Snake River as it cuts through Hells Canyon, the deepest river
gorge in North America, and drains the steep mountains between
Idaho and Oregon. I say probably because I'm piecing things
together from a sketch of the trip the woman felt compelled to
share in the form of a letter to the editor of an environmental
magazine.

Having visited this area, though, I can assure you it is a
sparsely populated land of intense beauty. The iconic Snake and
its tributaries carve through deep canyons and meander past high
meadows abutted by 9,000-foot peaks that are often compared to
the Alps. The topography can be vibrant and verdant with
lodgepole and larch, speckled with mountain lakes and
wildflowers, or it can be rugged and barren depending on elevation
and slope angle.

The speed limits are higher in Idaho, so the couple slips by
the southern reaches of the Wallowa-Whitman National Forest
and makes it to the border town of Ontario in less than two hours.
Ontario, with about 11,000 inhabitants, is the biggest city in
Malheur County, in all of eastern Oregon for that matter. Here,
they pick up Route 20 going west and glide between the southern
edge of Malheur National Forest and the northern boundary of the
Malheur National Wildlife Refuge.

This is high-desert scrubland, big buttes under big skies, a
hard land fit for coyotes, cougars, and cattle grazing. Most of it is
federally owned and operated by the Bureau of Land
Management. The refuge is where, in 2016, Ammon Bundy's

well-armed brigade of ranchers, sovereign-staters and tinfoil-hat wearers seized the park's headquarters in hopes of fanning the anti-government conflagration Ammon's father, Cliven, had set off at his Nevada ranch two years earlier. The flashpoint, ostensibly, was the $1 million in back fees Cliven owed for 20 years' worth of grazing cattle on public lands.

The real beef, though, is with what the refuge represents — the idea that the land is something other than a strictly utilitarian proposition, that the public has a stake in a region where cattle is king and public resources, nature even, have traditionally served special interests. There were probably better targets for the Bundy bunch's ire — Teddy Roosevelt created the Malheur Refuge to protect waterfowl from hunters — but in this one, and in other more recent conservation projects throughout the West, they could discern a growing threat to the generations of Manifest Destiny–salted entitlement around which their culture has cohered.

Four weeks into the Malheur occupation, one of the Bundy gang tries to run a roadblock and is shot and killed by federal officers. Ammon Bundy's brother, Ryan, suffers shrapnel wounds. The Bundy militants eventually surrender. Criminal charges, indictments and trials follow. A handful — along with their beliefs that the government was spraying chemtrails on citizens, that President Obama was not one of those citizens, that homosexuality was a disease and that the southern counties of Oregon should be an independent country — go to prison.

Not that long ago, this nonsense retained the whiff of the exotic. Now, we're inured to images of bearded men wielding unfortunate tattoos and long rifles at state houses and sandwich shops, railing against the tyranny of mask ordinances in the face of a deadly and highly communicable disease; railing against the social contract and the common weal.

In the early fall of 2011, however, as the motorcyclists roar past a refuge not yet under siege, we don't fully grasp how much farther down the road to suicidal stupidity we are yet to travel. We don't know that the couple enjoying Route 20 for all of its high-desert, blue-highway beauty is navigating another tributary that is rushing toward our current calamities.

Something else, though, a young wolf, is moving in the same direction, breaking path for a different destiny, one that we could still seize if we follow his lead.

At this point in his wanderings, he has gone too far to call this foray a restless walkabout. At this point, he is a disperser. One that has relinquished a sub-alpha role in the territory that his parents, OR-4 (the legendary fourth wolf captured and fitted with a GPS collar in Oregon) and B-300, had reclaimed just a few years prior by braving the Snake River and climbing into the Oregon side of the Hells Canyon Wilderness.

There, they found something wolves abhor — a bountiful and ready habitat devoid of wolves. There, they found the Zumwalt Prairie, North America's largest intact prairie grassland, a lingering remnant of the pre-cattle West teeming with elk and deer and, most importantly, lacking in humans. The pair started a pack near the confluence of the Imnaha River and Big Sheep Creek, just outside of Joseph. Wolves have been proliferating under the shadow of 9,838-foot Sacagawea Peak ever since.

By the fall of 2011, their son, OR-7, is halfway to California, stealing along a patchwork of public lands and open spaces, traveling a shadow infrastructure that has been stitched together by years of dogged environmental advocacy. This tenuous greenbelt just barely connects the Wallowa Mountains of his natal pack in the northeast of Oregon to the Cascades that run south and west down the spine of the state into California. By leaving those wild mountains and starting his trek just months before the motorcyclists start theirs, OR-7 is unwittingly proving the efficacy of linking up natural spaces into what environmentalists call wilderness corridors.

A public that becomes increasingly enamored with his lonesome wanderings will eventually give OR-7 the nickname "Journey." And though he is just the seventh Oregon wolf to be captured and fitted with a GPS collar, OR-7's lineage goes all the way back to the first few dozen wolves Carter Niemeyer brought here from backwoods Alberta, just a few years after I had been astonished by that wolf moseying along the train tracks.

Those wolves were released into Wyoming's Yellowstone National Park and Idaho's Frank Church–River of No Return Wilderness. The mid-'90s return of wolves to the northern Rocky Mountains, accomplished through a resolute application of the Endangered Species Act, is hard to top for dramatic and undertold stories of men and bureaucracy. It quickly turned into a proxy battle, the contours of which are all too familiar now, in the country's larger culture wars.

The anti-wolf lobby weaponized the rhetoric of paranoia, conspiracy and tribalism. They depicted wolves as dangerous, wanton creatures and called their reintroduction an act of Deep State treachery, an affront to "traditional" Western values. They prophesized ruination and promised retribution.

Underneath the hyperbole, they harbored deep existential anxieties. An ocean of blood had been spilled to take this land for "Americans," for their cows and their saws and their drills and their insatiable desire to subjugate. What was all that for if we were just going to return it to the vanquished? Where would it end?

Proponents of wolf reintroduction, on the other hand, pointed to the billions in subsidies that prop up otherwise untenable ranching and livestock concerns — industries that have damaged the environment more than cars ever will. In the return of wolves, they saw small but necessary steps toward curbing our appetites, restoring some equilibrium and extending the ethical sequence to include the land, much as Aldo Leopold proposed in his "Land Ethic" essay not long after examining his own regret for shooting a wolf on a mountain.

Leopold realized that a mountain without wolves is a dead mountain. For some, a land without wolves is a dead land. If you squinted hard enough, you could almost see in wolf reintroduction a modest pilot program for reparations aimed at amending some of the sins of Manifest Destiny.

All this baggage added up to gray wolves being brought back to the West under an unprecedented twisting of the Endangered Species Act. They were designated an experimental, nonessential species. This meant no habitat would be put aside for them (pointless in the case of wide-ranging wolves anyway) and that they'd be on their own after populations reached politically tenable, but scientifically dubious, numbers.

The ranching lobby's predictions of ruin haven't come true, of course. Wolves do kill livestock, but in statistically anomalous numbers. According to the USDA's industry-friendly stats, predators are responsible for just two percent of livestock deaths and wolves tally just a fraction of that. And while any animal loss is significant to individual ranchers, they are compensated when wolves are to blame. Negligence and disease kill the most cows by far, despite the billions of taxpayer dollars we pitch in for mending fences, clearing forests, dredging drainages, providing grazing lands, building culverts, dusting crops, enhancing pastures and generally doing what we can to keep the cheeseburger supply chain intact.

Far from ruinous, there is evidence that returning gray wolves to the West has indeed improved the environment, setting off what is called a trophic cascade of benefits. For example, Yellowstone's ecosystem had been suffering from prolific and complacent deer and elk populations that stripped entire swaths of the park clean. This was particularly egregious in the valleys where streambeds and riparian areas suffered from lack of cover and ecosystems collapsed. When wolves returned, they brought back a so-called ecology of fear, forcing prey to be alert and to move around more naturally. They put the wild back into the wilderness and overgrazed areas recovered.

The recriminations, on the other hand, were immediate. As gray wolves proliferated and moved farther west, they were met with calls to *shoot, shovel and shut up* and to *smoke a pack a day.* In the spring of 2011, just before OR-7 left his pack, federal protections for wolves in the Northern Rockies were lifted via a budget-bill rider. Many outside the livestock, hunting and logging lobbies viewed the move as an act of political expediency. As soon as they were let off the leash, states such as Montana, Idaho and Wyoming went back to killing wolves with prejudice.

***

At Bend, Oregon, the motorcyclists pick up Route 97 going south toward Crater Lake, where they spend the night. It's now early fall 2011 and OR-7 isn't even a rumor yet, let alone Journey, arguably the most famous wolf in the world. But he's been moving stealthily in the same direction as the motorcyclists, logging mile after mile along the edges of the human world, hidden by trees and shadows and tall grasses in open spaces.

The dangers are many — cars, crosshairs, a broken jaw — but this wolf is young, big and strong. He weighs more than 100 pounds and can easily travel 50 miles a day. For food, he might take over a lion's kill, or bring down a deer. He can make do with small mammals if needed. He's good at being a wolf.

The woman takes the lead out of Crater Lake in the morning en route to Upper Klamath Lake and the southern end of the Oregon Cascades. She isn't far down the road when an apparition flashes in front of her just as red and blue lights flash in her rearview mirror. She had forgotten about Oregon's ridiculous 55 mph speed limits, but that's not what's on her mind as the sheriff writes her up. She is transfixed by what she has just seen: a wolf crossing the road up ahead.

The deputy hands over the speeding ticket and tells her she's wrong, there are no wolves in these parts. But the woman knows wolves. Her hometown of McCall, Idaho, is an easy ride to the Frank Church–River of No Return Wilderness, and she was around when wolf B-13, just nine days after being repatriated from backcountry Canada to cattle country USA, trotted 60 miles north onto a rancher's spread and killed a calf. The wolf was shot through the heart and left to rot alongside the calf — the first two casualties in the wolf wars that have raged ever since.

A few months after the encounter with the cop, the woman's mother-in-law, who lives in Oregon City, sends her a newspaper clipping about a lone wolf spotted in the area where she and her husband had been riding their motorcycles. It wasn't a ghost she'd seen; it was OR-7.

Not long after that, just before Christmas 2011, OR-7 crosses into California. He dallies briefly in Siskiyou County on the state's northern border. As if to make a point, he moves on to Lassen County where the last of his California predecessors had been killed in 1924. The welcome wagon isn't exactly rolled out for the first wild gray wolf in California in 87 years. The supervisor of Siskiyou County tells the *Los Angeles Times* that she'd like to see any encroaching wolves shot on sight.

After looking like he was heading for Reno, GPS readings throughout the summer of 2012 show OR-7 doubling back and lingering around Lake Almanor in northern Plumas County. It's possible a massive wildfire in the region forced animals toward the lake and the wolf found the pickings easy.

Still, it's a curious place for him to be. Young wolves disperse in search of mates and OR-7 is now more than 600 miles as the crow flies from the nearest prospect. He has logged well over 1,000 miles in a quixotic quest only he seems to understand. As Journey's travels gain more attention and more admirers, the California Fish and Wildlife biologist who oversees his newly adopted territory cautions that this wolf is a goner, "a genetic dead end."

At home in Los Angeles, I have a different reaction. My imagination is still ripe and a wolf has once again captured it, filling my head with visions of a fierce-eyed dissident, a king of the forest coming to heal the land and maybe us in the bargain.

I jump in my car and head north. I'm not hoping to find OR-7 so much as I'm hoping to bear witness to the possibilities he represents — to find the map to the new world struggling to grow out of the smoldering ashes of the old one.

I follow his trail through our sclerotic arteries and into the boundaries of his new territory. I trace his steps into the hot summer timberlands of the northern counties on up through the wet, piney spine of autumnal Oregon. I go all the way to the snow-capped mountains whence he came. Nowhere in my travels do I find evidence of any great civilization that has risen from all the dammed rivers, scalped mountains, stripped valleys and spilled blood.

Instead, lonely logging trucks on winding passes, sandwich shops in one-stop towns, vacant mining shacks, railroad tracks and cows. I see nothing, not even in the great cities I skirt, that explains what all of the killing has been about. Nature, still insistent amid the charred husks, is the only thing.

And now, a lone wolf.

***

It's August 2014, an inflection point in California's epochal drought, and I'm driving north again. Somewhere, just after Interstate 5 winds through the steep rises, deep canyons and shallow valleys that give shape to the counties of Shasta and Siskiyou, the road curves around the towering hulk of Mount Shasta. It is here that the afternoon sun shrivels to a red dot and the sky darkens as if a thick fog is rolling in. One is not. It is smoke and ash from raging wildfires choking out the firmament, turning the landscape dull and gray.

Across the Oregon border, things start to look better. A massive dark cloud looms in the rearview mirror, but the sky ahead is blue and the late-afternoon sun is a familiar shape and color. The foothills and mountains recover a greener hue.

After 10 hours of driving, I arrive at Ashland where, despite its name, I can breathe without scarring my lungs. I check into a motel and walk around a little to get my legs under me. I have an appointment in the morning to see a man about a wolf.

OR-7 isn't alone anymore. Another wolf picked up his trail out of northeast Oregon and followed his tracks along the edges of humanity to the end of the state. They found each other near the Rogue River, south and west of Crater Lake near the Sky Lakes Wilderness, a region shaped by a collision of the wet coastal ranges with the drier inland Cascades. It's rife with water and vegetation. It seems perfectly designed to support life, and at five years old, near the end of the line for most wolves in the wild, the "genetic dead end" sired a litter of three pups here. The Rogue Pack became the first pack of wolves in western Oregon in more than six decades.

Their timing was uncanny. On the same day the Oregon Fish and Wildlife Service released the photos of the new wolf family, the California Fish and Game Commission was meeting to rule on whether or not gray wolves deserved protection under the state's Endangered Species Act. The proposal, inspired by OR-7's California adventuring, had looked bound for the floor when the California Department of Fish and Wildlife recommended against protecting wolves after OR-7 appeared to have settled north of the border. If there were no wolves in California, why protect them?

OR-7, though, had a knack for pranking bureaucrats. He crossed back into California on the very day the department made that recommendation. Then, on June 4, 2014, as the Game Commission met in Fortuna to make its final decision on the matter, photos of a new wolf pack just over the state line went viral. The room, stocked with wolf advocates, erupted in cheers. OR-7 forced the commission's hand and now gray wolves are under the protection of the California Endangered Species Act. So far, legal challenges by the California Cattlemen's Association and California Farm Bureau have failed.

OR-7 would go on to sire 12 pups in five consecutive litters between 2014 and 2018. One of OR-7's male offspring returned to his old haunts and started the Lassen Pack in 2017. The Lassen Pack is the only known wild wolf pack in California, though sporadic sightings of lone wolves following in OR-7's footsteps continue. This past spring, the pack added eight new pups. There are now fifteen known wolves in California. More wolves and packs are sure to come.

Wolves are protected in these parts, for now, but they are coming under increasing attack elsewhere. Last year, a ranch in Washington that grazes cattle on public land had 26 gray wolves killed for livestock depredation. The rancher said he believes the reintroduction of wolves is a plot to end private-enterprise cattle grazing on public lands. "I don't feel that we have room for wolves in Washington State," the rancher told *The Seattle Times*. "If it's allowed to continue, it's going to drive the ranching industry out of Washington, which is what a lot of people want. We're just stubborn, and we won't leave the range."

The return of wolves to our wilder spaces is far from settled, but OR-7 has arguably done more than any other wolf to give them a fighting chance. Fittingly, a biologist and lawyer with the Center for Biological Diversity, her tongue only slightly in cheek, dubbed him Messiah Wolf.

***

On the morning of my appointment, evidence of the inferno I'd driven through to get to the edge of the Sky Lakes Wilderness sits ominously over the southern border. The sky to the north, though, is mostly blue and I drive a few miles in that direction to meet up with Joseph Vaile, the executive director of the Klamath-Siskiyou Wildlands Center. Vaile is tall and boyishly handsome and would be played by John Krasinski in the movie. He has agreed to take me up into OR-7's territory. I guess I'm hoping for an audience with the messiah.

Vaile, a Midwesterner, tells me of growing up in a stultifying monoculture, a landscape long ago subjected to the floristic equivalent of gentrification. He studied biology in college and came out west to be around the last remnants of wild America — biological reservoirs in unaltered states, he called them.

As we gain altitude, the sky gets bluer and the trees greener and Vaile explains that we are in a vast eco-region of profound biodiversity, a geography of varied ranges, watersheds, topographies and microclimates that stretches west to the coast and south into the border counties that OR-7 patrolled during his years of living dangerously.

The land is a great habitat and coveted for its timber production, making it a source of much conflict and some compromise between conservationists and loggers. Organizations like Vaile's throughout Oregon and California have been fighting to protect these areas and add to them as they come under mounting stress from climate change, drought and extraction industries. By traveling from one end of Oregon to the other, and then on into California, and by establishing footholds for wolves everywhere he went, OR-7 proved the value of their efforts and fortified their arguments: land that can support wolves is land that has intrinsic worth…if for nothing else than seeding a comeback for wildlife after climate catastrophe.

We park at a trailhead and start hiking. About a mile up, past the tree farms, the forest turns thick with old-growth stands. Needles and cones cover the ground, birds chirp, and butterflies flutter. Critters scurry under fallen trees. The air feels fresh and new like it was on that morning in Alberta 25 years ago. Vaile says we are in OR-7's vicinity, but wolves' territories are huge and OR-7 is not nearly as interested in me as I am in him.

I don't encounter OR-7 or any other wolves, but I might have found what I was looking for, anyway: a glimpse of a future beyond the embers that have covered my car in soot by the time we get back down to the trailhead.

***

I had planned to go in search of OR-7 one last time, but the wolf that has taken up a storage shed's worth of my preoccupations went off the radar earlier this year just as the pandemic started laying bare so many of our misapprehensions.

Wolves don't harbor delusions, though, and OR-7 was exiled after his mate took up with a younger, stronger alpha. Eleven years old is ancient for a wolf in the wild and too old for a lone one. OR-7 is either dead or dying. It's probably just as well. A taste for cattle has turned the old wolf and his Rogue Pack into outlaws in recent years. It's messy here in the real world of wolves and men.

So, now, the pine needles that once padded his huge paws pull at him like quicksand. Now, the ravens and magpies that lived on his scraps look to see if his nostrils still flare. Now, the coyotes yip excitedly as news of the end of the big gray wolf from up north, the great disruptor, the great restorer, travels through the forest in the language of the forest.

He leaves as he came, a spectral figure tracing the liminal terrain between worlds, haunting us with the idea that we can either live with wolves, or die without them.

WRECKED

Originally published in the LA Weekly

So, I'm on my way back from my head doc around lunchtime, heading south on the 101 freeway over the Cahuenga Pass after having just paid $80 to learn that my pedestrian anxieties and run-of-the-mill insomnia stem from not feeling in control of things (revelatory!). I didn't sleep a wink last night, haven't eaten or had much to drink yet today and am feeling the aches from the surfing I did this morning before work. I'm delirious. Deliriously dreaming of the biggest burrito in the history of Poquito Mas, or maybe a double-double with fries from In-N-Out Burger, or Fatburger, in all its fatty-greasy splendor, for a change.

Endless possibilities await just a few hundred yards up the road, where the Barham exit will deliver me onto a stretch of fast-food heaven. After eating, I could even buy a car, any number of brands of car, if I were rich. Or I could get my film edited, if I had a film to be edited, or apply for a job at Vivid Entertainment, if I thought being a pornographer was the way to regain control of my life. It's really an embarrassment of riches on that stretch of Barham around the Cahuenga Pass. Hell, maybe I'd even move there.

The future is wide open, and it's going to start as soon as I make that exit.

Then, the future stops dead in its tracks. Not just for me, but for all four lanes of traffic, including the two highly cell-phoned black dudes in the Bentley sports coupe in front of me, the Pat Riley wannabe with the slicked hair and $1,000 suit driving the Mercedes SL500 next to them and the truck driver next to me. We wait for something to happen, something to move. Nothing does. It's really hot.

After a while, the slick-haired guy opens his car door and stands up on his floorboards to take a look. He turns to the guys in the Bentley and shakes his head. The Bentleys shake their heads back in mutual acknowledgment that *this kind of shit is for other people.*

I have my air conditioning on and notice I'm nearly out of gas. There's a service station within throwing distance, right there at the Barham exit. That damn exit is a portal to the world of the sentient. Down here, lined up like livestock on the 101, we are practically inert, unable to control our destinies. Crowds of real people start congregating up along the chain-metal fence separating the two worlds, gaping excitedly at us as if we're participants in some medieval sporting event.

We wait for something to change. I turn off my car to save gas, and start sweating profusely. I think I might pass out. One of the dudes gets out of his Bentley and starts working the cell phone. The Mercedes dude does the same. Four helicopters start buzzing overhead. I wonder if they'll be airlifted out. I need some water.

***

I get out of my car and start walking. *If I can just get to Barham.* I feel like Michael Douglas in *Falling Down*. I count more than a dozen emergency-personnel vehicles up ahead. Somehow a news crew has sprung up out of nowhere — just add disaster and voilà! There's bad shit going on up there, that's for sure, and nobody's getting near the Barham exit.

I walk over to the side of the road, scale a little incline and start to hop the fence. When my intentions become clear, the people on the other side eye me suspiciously but let me pass. I'm one of the Others, like from *Lost*. Even though I've made it to the land of free will, I'm not really free, since my car is still stuck in the miles of cars now lined up on the 101. I forgo a trip to Fatburger in favor of a quick dash to a nearby liquor store for water.

I hop back over the fence with my water and rejoin the ranks of the stuck. I look back at the wreckage. Firemen and EMTs scurry about. Someone's being put on a stretcher. It's awful. A newsbreak says the accident has traffic backed up past the 405 freeway.

I get in my car and sip the water. It's still really hot, and I'm parked directly beneath the sun. I notice the slick-haired guy walking back from the vicinity of the wreckage. He looks at the Bentley guys, and they instinctively seek solace in each other, communicating back and forth in the language of the normally exempt. Other motorists are out of their cars, bonding. Teens seem to find each other and huddle in clusters. A sense of being part of something has taken hold. I'm alone and roasting.

I get out of my car again and walk back toward the fence, where there's shade. As I approach, I notice a disheveled woman sitting on a bench in a grassy clearing on the other side of the fence. She's scribbling something furiously on a piece of brown paper.

"Whatcha doing?" I ask.

"Putting a cover on my AA book," she tells me. Her hair is matted, and her two front teeth may be implants suffering from extreme neglect. Her clothes are dirty, but her figure's kind of held up.

"Remember how you used to do that in elementary school?" she asks.

She tells me she likes to put covers on all her books and produces the one she's going to do next, a dime-store romance novel by the looks of it.

"I got these from the Burbank Library," she says, and starts digging through her purse until she finds her wallet. "See, here's my library card. I just got that the other day. And here's my Ralphs card, and here's my . . ." She shows me every card in her wallet.

"What are you doing all the way over here if your library is in Burbank?" I ask.

"I had my anger-management class," she says. "I'm also taking physics. My professor is really good. I'm good at physics."

I ask how AA is going.

"Really good, bro. I used to do a lot of dope. But I've been off it for three years. Except for three relapses."

I wonder if this is one of them. "That's great," I say, smiling through the fence.

"I've seen you before," she says, while carefully folding what appears to be a blond wig and placing it in some kind of mesh bag. "I noticed you over there. You looked calm and I knew you'd come over here."

She pulls a brush from her bag and starts brushing her real hair, which is short and dark. She's sort of attractive, in a tough-luck, dual-diagnosed kind of way. Once, though, she must have been somebody's baby.

"Hey," she says, "if you ever want to get out of here, I know when the spaceships are coming."

Up ahead, the emergency vehicles start moving out.

"Thanks," I said. "I gotta get back to my car. You take care."

"You too, bro."

Traffic begins to move. The future is wide open.

PART TWO

They Could Be Heroes

"Becoming a man is hard stuff. You're not born into it; you arrive at it through loss, struggle and determination."

IT'S ALWAYS DARKEST BEFORE THE DAWN

Tommy Caldwell, Kevin Jorgeson and the world's toughest free climb

Originally published in Huck Magazine

Drive into Yosemite National Park from the West and the great slab of rock called El Capitan rises in all its burnished glory so quickly and so definitively one wonders if John Muir, the park's legendary godfather, arranged things so visitors would be inspired to get the hell out of their cars. Luckily, there's a meadow along the road that splays out before the 3,000-foot, near-vertical monolith making it easy enough for humans to grab a quick slice of humble pie before venturing farther into the park.

Though winter is off-season in Yosemite, the meadow has hosted more guests than usual this season as spectators gathered to gaze through binoculars at two men engulfed in a dramatic quest to free-climb El Capitan's Dawn Wall, rated by those who know as the most difficult big-wall free climb in the world. Tommy Caldwell and Kevin Jorgeson had been failing miserably at this pursuit for years, but through the miracle of social media, and perhaps because the world is in dire need of things to cheer for, this particular attempt captured the imagination of folks who had never picked up a climbing magazine and likely never will.

A week after their attempt, Caldwell and Jorgeson are wolfing down large cheeseburgers in the vast dining hall of the Ahwanhee Hotel in the heart of Yosemite Village. Caldwell and Jorgeson look slightly amiss in their worn jeans and flannels, unkempt facial hair and tattered, abused hands that look unfit to pick up a salad fork, let alone grip and hold on to a wart-sized piece of stone jutting from a sheer wall that could spell the difference between rising or falling.

When we meet for lunch, the men are on a break between sessions for a *Vanity Fair* photo shoot. It's been like this — a parade of interviews, morning-show appearances and, well, *Vanity Fair* shoots — since they got back to ground after nearly three weeks of pressing their noses, backs, arms, hands and feet into the unforgiving face of El Capitan's Dawn Wall.

"I can't imagine two more polar opposite worlds than living on the wall for 19 days and coming down to 3:30 press conferences," says Jorgeson, whose thick black hair, high cheekbones and intense eyes would seem to make him a fine choice to be the new face of modern climbing, if there is to be such a thing. "That's about as far apart from one another as it gets."

Not that they're not grateful for the opportunities that are sure to come from their newfound celebrity. After all, it wasn't long ago that Jorgeson was living out of his van. But it's pretty clear this isn't their scene. Their scene is way up high where they can be just specks on the grand canvas, invisible to the naked eye.

***

Tommy Caldwell is just 36, but the weathered lines around his eyes read like a trail map of a well-traveled life. He has a sort of quiet, soulful intensity about him. Mostly, he loves to climb.

"I crave climbing like I crave food or water. If I don't have it, I feel like something's missing," says Caldwell. "I crave the adventure that isn't part of normal, everyday life anymore, and climbing is an outlet that you can do in a relatively safe way that fulfills those needs and gets you out into this natural world and brings us back to the way we're built as human beings."

Before he embarked on the journey that has made him and Jorgeson arguably big-wall climbing's first-ever household names, the Patagonia-sponsored climber had been quietly racking up First Free Ascents (FFAs) on El Cap, including Lurking Fear, Magic Mushroom and other routes. In 2004, he did an FFA on Dihedral Wall and followed that up the next year by free-climbing The Nose (on which he'd previously made the third ascent), descending East Ledges and then ascending Freerider, all within 24 hours. That, too, was a first.

Despite the audacity of his efforts in Yosemite and elsewhere, something started haunting him in the way it would haunt a true climber: the Dawn Wall, so called because the morning light bleeds down its face from top to bottom as the sun rises. "I'd climbed different routes on El Cap for 12 years before I even considered that the Dawn Wall was possible," says Caldwell. "We're always searching for the limit of what we can do, where we can take climbing. Once we got to know El Cap well, we'd look at that wall and be like, 'Is this possible?'"

Not many thought it was. The route up Dawn Wall would require scaling some of the hardest climbing pitches in the world, with the two hardest in a back-to-back sequence. Simply put, it was widely regarded as the most difficult free climb in the world. But once a new route gets in a climber's mind, it tends to nag like a psychic itch.

From 2003 to 2010, Caldwell was married to Beth Rodden, a world-class climber in her own right. The two met on the sport-climbing circuit in the mid-'90s when they were teenagers winning every competition in sight. Before long, they were climbing's first couple. In fact, they are the subjects of a 2006 film called *The First Couple of Rock*. The Dawn Wall itch became an obsession when that marriage began to break up.

Caldwell says the breakup was his first taste of failure and he initially had trouble accepting it wasn't a problem he could solve. "I'm so obsessive about things that once I get on that track, I just stick with it until I do it. Failing in a marriage just isn't that. I couldn't control that at all," says Caldwell, who is now happily remarried and the proud father of a 20-month-old boy.

"I had this vision for it before I went through my divorce and then in that time, when my mind was going a million miles an hour and I was in this really crazy state, I needed a distraction from the pain of that," he adds. "That's when I really took this project on full force, because being up there in this place that I love and working hard was kind of the only time I could feel normal for a while."

If the divorce fueled his fire to take on a daunting challenge, Caldwell can thank another traumatic event for the preternatural calm he displays in the face of such challenges.

When the fall of the Soviet Union opened up the former republics to the world, Kyrgyzstan's remote Kara Su valley in the Pamir Alai Range became an international climbing destination along the lines of Yosemite. In the summer of 2000, Caldwell and Rodden were the junior members of a four-person expedition that included American climbers Jason "Singer" Smith and John Dickey. They planned to tackle Yellow Wall, a 2,500-foot headwall ascent on 12,000-foot Mount Zhioltaya Stena.

On the second day of their four-day ascent, the group was taken captive by fundamentalist guerrillas from the Islamic Movement of Uzbekistan. The ordeal that followed — six days of freezing, starving, witnessing executions and surviving crossfires — has been recounted by writer Greg Child in his gripping piece for *Outside* magazine, "Fear of Falling."

Convinced they'd die at the hands of their captors, the group's opportunity for salvation came one night when they were left under the watch of just one man. Caldwell, who until that point would have seemed the least likely candidate, seized the moment and pushed the man off a ledge high up in the remote mountains. The group fled to a Kyrgyz army base miles away.

Caldwell says the ripple effects of that experience have been profound for all four members of the expedition, and that it inevitably factored into the breakup of his marriage. But, he adds, it also left him some gifts. "Life is so valuable and the Kyrgyzstan experience brought that into the front of my mind. It made me push so hard on everything else because it made life tangible. I know I can't take it for granted."

As far as how it affected his climbing, Caldwell says, "In a lot of regards, that experience was so intense and painful and life-threatening, it just turned up the volume so much that everything since then has felt comparatively mellow. I can go up on El Cap and be in storms, or have crazy stuff happening — Kevin's seen it. Other people are scared and I'm like, 'Well, this isn't really that big of a deal,' because I have that to compare it to."

***

While Caldwell was working out his issues on various Dawn Wall pitches, Jorgeson was busy making daring first ascents in the climbing discipline of highball bouldering — scaling large, freestanding rocks without the aid of ropes, bolts or other climbing aids.

In January 2009, Jorgeson's first ascent of Ambrosia, a 45-foot face on the Grandpa Peabody boulder in the Buttermilks of the Eastern Sierras, blurred the lines between super-highball bouldering and the do-or-die discipline of free solo climbing. Though it became his signature ascent, the experience left Jorgeson wondering where the hell he was going with all this. "Ambrosia could have been fatal if you fell in the wrong place for sure," he says. "I felt that if I raised the bar again, I'd be free soloing, where it's certain death if you fall, and that's not a discipline I'm that interested in."

After Ambrosia, Jorgeson began seeking a new direction. Meanwhile Caldwell, after years spent on various Dawn Wall pitches, was having second thoughts about the feasibility of a continuous free-climb push. In fact, he'd just about given up and decided to release a film of his failed 2009 attempt just so "we could show the climbing world what the future is, because I didn't think that I'd ever be able to do it."

Despite the failure of that attempt, Caldwell had a good time with his friends on the film crew, which led to a revelation. "I was like, man, if the Dawn Wall can be done with good people all up there together having this cool adventure, maybe that's what I need."

Jorgeson saw the film and thought, "Whoa, it kind of looks like he needs a partner." It was a match made in heaven except for one small problem: Jorgeson had never done big-wall climbing before. In fact, before Dawn Wall, he'd never climbed El Cap, or any other Yosemite milestone for that matter.

"The first day that he came to Yosemite, we put on 75-pound packs and walked to the top of El Cap, which is 3,000 feet up steep slabs. It's physically a really, really hard thing that would crush most people," recalls Caldwell, "and Kevin, having not really been in that world much at all, he got to the top and threw down his pack and said, 'Yeah, that felt good!' And I was like, this is awesome! Then, we rappelled off El Cap to what is probably the most exposed spot in North America. Most people get vertigo when they go up there and immediately we were trying to figure out the top of the route, because it was a section that I hadn't looked at and we're having to take these giant swings across the wall to try and find the holes . . . and this was day one. Day one of Kevin joining in the project!"

Jorgeson's eyes light up. "What a cool experience," he says. "I mean, I grew up seeing Tommy in magazines. To be taken on this project — I would have done anything."

Caldwell and Jorgeson's route up Dawn Wall comprised 31 pitches. A pitch is the distance between a starting point and a resting point on the ascent. It's always within the length of the climbers' safety ropes — 200 feet or less.

When the two attempted a push on Dawn Wall in 2010, Jorgeson couldn't make Pitch 12 and the climb stopped after seven days. For that matter, prior to this attempt, Jorgeson had never done Pitch 12, or 14 or 16, some of the hardest pitches on their route. Caldwell had tackled each pitch on the route, just not in a continuous free-climb push.

They'd been working this project for six years now with countless falls and frustrations as well as the odd breakthrough here and there to sustain them. The forecast for the end of December was too good to not give it another go. If they were going to be successful on this attempt, Jorgeson would just have to figure out some things on the fly.

It started well and by their second day on the wall — day six of the push — troublesome Pitch 12 was behind them and so was Pitch 14, the one they thought would be the hardest.

"We'd get to pitches and we'd do them quickly, whereas in the past, we'd failed so much. It started this ball rolling that was extraordinary. Basically until Pitch 15," Caldwell says, and then laughs.

"Tommy's roll didn't stop," Jorgeson adds. "Well, it stopped at 20 because he was waiting for me, but mine hit the wall at Pitch 15." At that point, the route's sharp points had punctured Jorgeson's fingers, making it impossible to get traction on Pitch 15's tiny holds. He tried to find ways around the problem, but fell time and again.

Meanwhile, Caldwell was at Pitch 20, the most difficult parts of the climb behind him. By then, *The New York Times* had written about their attempt and NPR interviewed them from their portaledge at 1,500. The world was tuning in on Twitter and Facebook. The pressure was mounting on Jorgeson.

He tried everything to get his skin to mend — Neosporin wraps, spray-on skin, tape from Australia. He stared at his fingers and willed them to heal. Seven torturous days had gone by and he was still stuck at Pitch 15.

"It was kind of a bummer," he says, deadpan.

Finally, he had the idea to ask the crew filming their attempt to compile his falls and post them on Vimeo so he could study them.

"Essentially what clicked was I watched a bunch of videos of all my failed attempts," says Jorgeson. "I have a memory for sequences and stuff, so I remembered what it felt like on each of those sequences when I fell. And I remembered this insecurity with my right foot, which you're parked on and you have to have the utmost confidence in."

On his next attempt, Jorgeson made a slight adjustment on a small foothold and made it through the pitch. Soon, he was reunited with Caldwell at Pitch 20.

On January 14, 19 days after they started, the two men finished the world's hardest free climb together.

"We failed at this for a lot of years and we stuck with it until it happened," says Caldwell. "One of the things that's been so cool about this is that we went all in on something that we didn't know if we could do. We were just really following our hearts and it worked out. It strengthened that inside me . . . that if there's something your heart tells you that you should do, you should go for it."

FATHER POP

How Mike Salisbury defeated communism
with sex, drugs and rock and roll

Originally published in The Surfer's Journal

It's noon somewhere, but not at the Venice Beach bar where Mike Salisbury sits in a corner booth, absently spooning ice cubes into a glass of white wine. At 73, time and motorcycle injuries have softened the lines that made him movie-star handsome not too long ago. Still, dressed like Johnny Cash in sweats, Salisbury has presence. On this gray, workday morning, while a handful of regulars and the sound system aspire to a Friday night, he quietly tells stories of his remarkable career in a zigzag, digressive fashion. It's as if his long, rich life has burst at the seams and golden nuggets are spilling out all over the place.

One of those nuggets has to do with that red-hot minute in the 1960s when Salisbury lived on Balboa Island in a small apartment with Randy Nauert. This is significant because a half dozen years or so before, Nauert had taught his high-school buddy Rick Griffin how to surf. Griffin lived up the road in Palos Verdes. Meanwhile, John Van Hamersveld was residing in the instant-kitsch glory of the Hollywood Riviera Apartments, just blocks from Torrance Beach, where he would meet Griffin to surf.

Talk about formative.

Salisbury, Griffin and Von Hamersveld spent their time at day jobs muddling through Chouinard Art Institute (later CalArts), surfing and scraping by while Nauert got busy working on the sound he'd been exploring since high school, something that would later be called surf music.

Times were good and times were tight. Salisbury says they "lived on oranges and avocados picked off the groves, cheap beer and cheaper chuck steaks with mac and cheese when it was really lean."

These guys had been drawing cartoons, painting, pinstriping and internalizing *Mad* magazine since junior high. Now, they were making posters for their friends' bands, logos for local shapers, and graphics for surf shops. Everything was just starting out.

Their budding talents converged around *Surfer* magazine when Nauert introduced Griffin to John Severson after *Surf Fever* screened at Nathaniel Narbonne High in Harbor City. Griffin debuted his seminal *Murphy* cartoon in *Surfer*, Van Hamersveld came on as an assistant and a designer and Salisbury did a bit of everything — art direct, ad design, report, write and contribute his own cartoons and illustrations, especially when the deadline-challenged Griffin fell behind.

Doing "everything" would become a Salisbury trademark, but what he did better than most was the right thing at the right time. Like putting Murphy on the cover of the August-September 1962 issue of *Surfer*, a move that both sealed the effervescent grem's fate as perhaps the first avatar of a nascent surf culture and provided *Surfer* with a proprietary identity. "People got that cover tattooed on their arms," laughs Nauert.

These guys would leave a few more marks on the landscape. Nauert was soon to take advantage of two technological advances — the Fender electric bass and the Fender Showman amp (reverb!) — to help create the sound of surf music with the Challengers, whose 1962 debut album, *Surfbeat*, would become the biggest-selling surf-rock record of all time.

Griffin, who did most of the Challengers' early artwork, moved to San Francisco a couple years later where his album covers and concert posters for the Grateful Dead and other Haight-Ashbury staples would help define the visual vocabulary of the psychedelic '60s.

Van Hamersveld was just a year or so away from creating the iconic *The Endless Summer* poster, a detonation that would catapult him into a career fashioning some of the more persistent imagery of our lifetimes, including the *Magical Mystery Tour* and *Exile on Main St.* album covers, the official Los Angeles Summer Olympics posters and mural and, of course, the Fatburger logo.

For a while, Salisbury cut a more modest profile. He produced the cover art for Dick Dale and the Del-Tones' debut, *Surfers' Choice*, and the logos and ads for regional outfits such as Ramsey Jay, Gordon & Smith and Birdwell Beach Britches. But in the coming years and decades, his impact on our postwar pop culture and identity would be immense, if not always obvious. "You don't see Mike, you see his work," says Nauert. "He shaped how we saw everybody else. He was like the architect."

What Salisbury was building, if you get right down to it, was an idea, one of the most powerful ideas of the past 60 years — the idea of California. He would use that idea to fight communism. California would win.

***

Before we get to how Salisbury won the Cold War, let's go back to the hot one that preceded it. In 1943, Salisbury was born into a Mayflower family with a military bent. His father was in the Army Air Corps, lots of uncles in the service, a cousin who was a highly decorated Vietnam Marine vet. Salisbury himself had a congressional appointment to Annapolis but turned it down. "I'd been on so many ships in my life, I just couldn't see being on a ship," he says. "All gray with that smell of diesel all the time."

His life at sea came courtesy of his stepfather, a Navy man whose career dealt Salisbury a peripatetic childhood. They moved to Long Beach from San Francisco when Salisbury was in the first grade, leaving the gray, dense city up north for a wonderland of tract homes, rides on the Red Car and a perpetually shining sun. It made an impression.

"The girls had bows in their hair and the men wore T-shirts with the sleeves rolled up, cigarettes balancing on their lower lips," recalls Salisbury. "We had motor scooters and motorcycles and old jalopies and a neighbor had one of the first TVs, which all of us kids would watch sitting cross-legged on the floor."

In Southern California, the future had arrived. Families that weren't military worked in aerospace. Salisbury would attend jet-fighter test flights. The aesthetic differences between the two major geographies of his childhood were keenly observed.

"In Southern Californian design and architecture, it is all streamline, space age," he says. "San Francisco is very Victorian and New York, very gothic. Greater L.A. was the new world. Cars were customized to look streamline. Houses were new and modern. Restaurants were drive-ins with towers replicating the Einstein Tower in Potsdam. New was not wrong. Every kid had to have the latest and most faddish. Consumerism began in earnest in Southern California. More was not enough."

Salisbury counts 11 moves in his first 11 years. Back to San Francisco for the fourth grade, then Monterey Bay while his stepfather attended the Naval Postgraduate School. At age 10, Salisbury lived in naval barracks across the Hawaiian Islands before the family set sail for the Marshalls.

When the first hydrogen bomb was tested off Bikini Atoll 1,000 miles away, Salisbury says the women and children weren't aware what was happening. Instead, they were put in shelters the day of the blast and told there might be a tidal wave. "But we escaped the shelter and swam and spear-fished and collected coral and shells at low tide on the reefs that were the tops of the volcanic cones that made the atoll and that wave never appeared."

Salisbury's family made it back to Southern California and the Long Beach suburb of Lakewood in time for junior high and high school. Lakewood then was an exemplar of postwar planned communities, offering the illusion of a *Leave It to Beaver* existence for the middle-class. Except, Salisbury says, he and his peers were dressing like Marlon Brando in *The Wild One* and acting like they were starring in *The Concrete Jungle*.

Attracted to such counter-narratives, Salisbury says he would ride his bike over to George Barris' studio in Lynwood every day to study Von Dutch. Soon, he was pinstriping everything from his notebooks to his bike to the furniture in his room. He drew cartoons for the school paper, caricatures for the yearbook and naked women and cars for himself and his friends. He got attention for his drawings. "Especially from the girls," he says.

This was the dawn of Kalifornia Kool — surf, hotrods, lowbrow art, rebellion from suburban anesthesia — and Salisbury wasn't there to be an observer.

***

We meet up again at the same bar a few days after our first encounter. It's still not noon and the bar is still too eager with wide doors inviting in the foggy cold and a sound system stuck on a Friday night. This is the new, friendly Venice Beach and Salisbury has been living here in a three-story townhome just a few blocks away since 1998.

It was different when he was coming. "Did you see *Inherent Vice*?" he asks, voice barely audible over the din. "It really is a picture of what it was like in the '70s. You had all this wild vice, but if you needed money, you could get money and have a job because there was so much in the entertainment business to make money off."

By 1974, Salisbury had already established himself as a creative force in Los Angeles and was hot off a stint as art director of the fabled *West* magazine when he got tapped by Jann Wenner to completely redesign *Rolling Stone* from its rigid newspaper-style inception into its more freewheeling and familiar tabloid incarnation. The first day on the job, Salisbury says, Wenner called him into his office, peered across a large oak table, and said, "You gotta fire Annie Leibovitz. She's costing me too much money."

According to Salisbury, Leibovitz had a penchant for abandoning rental cars wherever she hopped out of them and burning through tons of film. She wasn't easy or cheap, but Salisbury knew firing Leibovitz would be suicide. "I said, 'She's the key to what that magazine is all about, which is rock and roll stars.'" Instead, Salisbury had an idea that would give them more bang for their buck and didn't hurt Leibovitz's career, either. "I'll make the pictures bigger," he decided.

Back then, Salisbury commuted to San Francisco from Los Angeles, due in no small part to *Rolling Stone*'s work habits — long lulls broken up by three days of deadline mayhem. When their backs were really against the wall, a woman in a nurse's uniform walked around, "giving everybody speed to stay up," says Salisbury. "There was no way I was going to sit up there while they got their shit together."

Salisbury quit *Rolling Stone* and opened up a Los Angeles office to focus on his growing branding business, a business that would eventually help reinvent Michael Jackson, make Levi's 501s a household name, add the Paris to L'Oreal, design album covers for Randy Newman, James Taylor, George Harrison and many more, as well as create campaigns for more than 300 movies including *Rocky IV*, *Silkwood*, *Raiders of the Lost Ark*, *Aliens* and *Jurassic Park*. Salisbury would package Bubble Yum, brand Halo and redesign *Playboy*, *Hustler*, *Penthouse* and *Surfing* magazines several times over. There'd be almost no corner of the American psyche his work hadn't wormed its way into by the turn of the century.

But, in 1975, he just wanted a break from magazines. Then, the phone rang at his new office. "The first call I answer is, 'Hello, this is Francis Coppola, I've got a magazine and George Lucas said I should hire you to art direct.'"

Coppola flew Salisbury, his wife and son up to San Francisco in his Mitsubishi Turboprop and sent around a metallic, light-blue Mercedes stretch to fetch them up to his Pacific Heights mansion. "Nicholas Cage opens the door," says Salisbury. "Jimmy Caan is playing the piano and George Lucas was there and [Coppola's] sister, Talia Shire, and his father, who did all the music for *The Godfather*, and his mother was busy in the kitchen making dinner."

The magazine was *City* and Salisbury recruited legendary Ramparts editor Warren Hinckle to help get it launched. One attention-grabbing cover featured the rhetorical statement "Why Women Can't Get Laid in S.F." across the bottom of the page just below a photograph of a leggy woman in a barely-there dress looking bemused while two disinterested men talk at a bar behind her.

"What I do is create metaphors," says Salisbury. "Visual metaphors mostly."

***

Metaphors, tricks of communication by which difficult concepts are made easy through the magic of symbolism. The world is a stage. A white whale is dread. And Murphy is the everyman who surfs or dreams of it.

Before Salisbury began trafficking in metaphors, he dropped out of USC to stay with his folks, who had finally settled in Oceanside for its proximity to the amenities of Camp Pendleton. In those days, Salisbury worked for an architect and design firm and surfed Pacific Beach, La Jolla Shores and Sunset Cliffs on a 9'3" Gordon & Smith in the winter with no leash. In his downtime, he hung around the surf shops and traded logo work — Gordon & Smith, Bobby Thomas' Challenger surfboards, Billy Caster — for boards and bread.

"Did you ever read *The Pump House Gang*? That's where I started surfing, with those guys. There was this great outlaw side to surfing. It didn't have the best image when John [Severson] came out with the magazine . . . a heavy job was to make that magazine get a broader appeal," says Salisbury. "And that was one of the reasons he got Murphy in there."

The question was how to broaden the product's appeal while maintaining and enhancing its inherent cool. Salisbury solved that problem with just about everything he did, from *Surfer* to early ad work for Birdwell Beach Britches to Levi's to Gotcha years later.

"I created what I felt were very sophisticated ads for them," says Salisbury.

After *Surfer* and a short stint at *Playboy*, Salisbury began seriously honing his chops at Carson Roberts, the most creative advertising agency on the West Coast in the mid-'60s. There, he worked alongside Ed Ruscha, future TV personality Joel Siegel, and future Monty Python trouper Terry Gilliam.

This was in the late '60s, when Otis Chandler had finally wrestled control of the *Los Angeles Times* from his über-conservative forebears and set about reimagining the paper for the modern world. To that end, Chandler hired Jim Bellows, the legendary *New York Herald Tribune* editor and patron saint of new journalism. At the *Tribune*, Bellows started what would become *New York* magazine, the hip alternative to the fussier *New York Times Magazine* and *The New Yorker*. Bellows, upon the recommendation of Siegel, who had been writing some for the

Times, approached Salisbury to art direct a similar *Los Angeles Times* initiative called *West* magazine.

"Everyone said, you can't go there, because it's this staid, republican paper," Salisbury recalls. "I said, 2 million people will see me every Sunday and I get to do anything I want."

With cutting-edge magazines such as Britain's *Nova* and Germany's *Twen* as touchstones, Salisbury proceeded to produce content and cover images that many still view as the apotheosis of West Coast publishing. Among them were an unfinished freeway ramp rising like a giant single fin into the sky, Von Dutch painting the *West* logo on a motorcycle's gas tank, the "Goodbye Ed Sullivan" cover with a tear coming from the CBS eye.

The concepts were instantly iconographic — meta and metaphorical — and they spoke volumes about a misread and underestimated city that was coming fast onto the world stage. In many ways, *West* provided the first second look at Los Angeles.

By the dawn of the '80s, surfing had the same issue — it needed a second look. By then, it had grown from a cloistered activity supplied out of bay-city garages to a regional cottage industry to something on the verge of being a global phenomenon. However, following the first wave of tongue-in-cheek kitsch and the second wave of action-based imagery, it seemed to have run out of interesting things to say about itself.

"Surfing had an image that wasn't being serviced by the graphics that represented it," says Michael Tomson, co-founder of Gotcha.

Surfing creative had grown safe and stale and Tomson was eager to boost his Gotcha brand with a vibe that would appeal to kids coming up on punk rock, MTV and increasing globalization. He called on Salisbury, who summoned his *Pump House Gang* roots for inspiration.

Salisbury's work for Gotcha, and later OP and O'Neill, was infused with punk-rock energy, animated color palettes, distressed text and Peter Beard–inspired collaging. They told stories that took place out of the water as much as in it, stories about boys and girls and sex and cool. They were stories you could place yourself in, even if you didn't live near a beach. To a large degree, the industry rode those stories into department stores across the world and Gotcha rose from zero to a $100 million company in less than a decade.

"We did some spectacular shit," says Tomson.

***

One of the landmarks of Salisbury's career was Michael Jackson's *Off the Wall* album cover. Salisbury had seen Jackson in *The Wiz* and came away convinced he was the next big thing. "I know his manager from UA [United Artists] and I call him up and say, 'Look, you gotta let me work on something for this kid. He's gonna be huge.'"

Jackson happened to have a solo album in the bag, but nobody liked the cover. So, Salisbury headed over to Freddy DeMann's office for a peek. "It looked like it was for the Sears children's department," says Salisbury. "I said, 'Let's put him in a tuxedo,' because I wanted him to come out with this album like he's Frank Sinatra . . . he's not a kid anymore."

Salisbury says DeMann wasn't quite getting it, when "all of a sudden, there's this little squeaky voice from the back — there are these floor-to-ceiling curtains — and from behind the curtains comes this little voice, '*I like it*.'"

When Jackson later came up with the sequin-glove idea, Salisbury suggested he wear just one.

Those Levi's ads that used iconic shots of Steve McQueen, Pete Townshend, Bruce Springsteen, and the Ramones in jeans, and put them on the side of buildings, were also Salisbury's handiwork. In fact, when Salisbury was handling Levi's creative while he was with Foote, Cone & Belding, he created the 501 brand name.

At the time, Levi's didn't have a traditional five-pocket women's jean to compete with Jordache and jailbait Brooke Shields' Calvin Kleins. But Salisbury knew the cool chicks were taking Levi's basics for men and shrinking and tailoring them. The stock number for the men's basic was 501. That's how people out in the world asked for Levi's — *do you have any 501s?*

"I said register the name 501 as a brand name and we'll say, *Now Cut for Women, 501*," says Salisbury.

He designed a logo and then came up with the print and TV campaign, a takeoff on jean-clad James Dean in *Giant* kicking his boots over the front seat of that big, black car. "I said, I'll do that, but with a woman." The "Travis, You're a Year Too Late" ads were a sensation and pretty soon every woman had a pair of 501s.

***

Filmmaker Doug Pray (*Surfwise, Hype*) recently started a documentary that attempted to tackle the question of Mike Salisbury and his impact on our lives. It quickly became clear to Salisbury, though, that a pithier approach was needed — a metaphor. From the abandoned doc, he came up with the idea of a TV show — *Mr. Pop Culture: The true story about the birth of pop culture and the CIA operative who engineered it.*

The trailer for *Mr. Pop Culture* begins with Salisbury's disembodied head in black and white against a solid black background. "I'm Mike Salisbury," the head says, "and I fought communism with sex, drugs and rock and roll."

Next, John Lennon primal-screams us into the Beatles' "Revolution" while images from Salisbury's life and work careen by — Hunter S. Thompson, *Rolling Stone*, *Playboy*, Pipeline, Andy Warhol, Camel Joe, hotrods, Hot Wheels, Bubble Yum, Halo, Levi's, Harrison Ford, Francis Coppola, Dick Dale, *Aliens* . . . and on and on.

It's a mind-blowing barrage of postwar iconography and it all traces back to the one place, the epochal source of all these other metaphors. "People over there wanted to live like us and they wanted to be like us," says Salisbury, "like Californians, really."

The trailer ends with fuchsia and white text stating the obvious: *communism didn't stand a chance.*

FUTURE MAN

Originally published in The Surfer's Journal

Take Las Virgenes Road from the 101 freeway and drive into the heart of Malibu Canyon past hoary Mulholland and keep going to Piuma Road. Then, take a left and climb through the rolling hills up toward the mountain peaks and find Las Flores Canyon Road, the downward glide of which will take you to the sea-breeze side of the slope and the easy-to-miss cul-de-sac where Jim Evans lives. Getting there is the stuff of "Dead Man's Curve" nightmares. Kids high on downhill skateboarding daredevilry pass going one way while ninjas on rice rockets scream by going the other. Overhead, red-tail hawks interrupt an otherwise spotless blue sky. It's a perfect afternoon for Malibu mythmaking.

Maybe too perfect. The next hairpin summons slowdowns and sirens as EMTs tend to a would-be hero, crashed and burned by the side of the road while his weekend-warrior buddies look on aghast. There's nothing to do but offer a prayer and climb, baby, climb. This is Southern California, after all, and legends are hard won if at all.

The drive to Evans' house reminds me of something Jacqueline Miro — the editor, urban planner and, most pertinently, *Swell* exhibit co-curator — said about Evans himself in a recent conversation. *Swell*, which had a nice 2010 run at Nyehaus Gallery in Manhattan, was one of the more recent — and better — attempts by the Empire City to come to terms with 60 years of the

Exploding California Inevitable, aka surf culture. In putting together the show — which featured Evans, Craig Stecyk, Ed Ruscha, Billy Al Bengston, Sandow Birk and many more — Miro was drawn to the sense of adventure and expansiveness she found among the Golden State's art and artists.

"There's a sense of courage and character-building on the West Coast that find lacking in New York City," says Miro. "This runs from Jim Evans to Billy Al Bengston to Ed Moses and it's something I admire very much."

As for Evans, on whom we'll be spending most of our time here, Miro succinctly nails the source of his enduring relevance.

"There's just so much history I love that Jim's been a part of."

For Miro, a Salvadoran who grew up surfing from the age of nine before moving on to headier pursuits such as studying architecture at Tulane and getting her graduate degrees in Paris, it was an early '90s Jane's Addiction piece that led her down the rabbit hole that ended up with Jim Evans in New York as one of *Swell*'s stars.

"These posters were so powerful in my mind. He became a Gerry Lopez to me, something of that quality," she explains. "Jim, as an artist, has the ability to capture the zeitgeist of whatever decade he's portraying. Whether he's doing surf or grunge or *The Hunger Games* today, he gets the essence of that time. He really does believe that what surrounds a certain movement is as important as what's being produced."

***

Postwar Southern California is easy to imagine but harder to grasp.

A new generation of Midwesterners, among them James Leroy Evans — a scrappy kid from Chicago who enlisted at the age of 17 when Pearl Harbor was attacked — arrived for boot camp, got a quick glimpse of sun, surf and palm trees, was quickly shipped off from Camp Pendleton to Midway, Guadalcanal and Iwo Jima. When they came back, these kids brought with them the influences of the wider world to which Southern California was the new portal.

As they settled in to raise families, the now-mighty Southern California military-industrial complex brought with it a pervasive cultural schizophrenia: a newfound prosperity fraught with an entirely new nuclear anxiety. California was suddenly both the beginning and the beginning of the end. And meanwhile, all the violence of bloody war in the Pacific festered like an infection just beneath the skin.

What's a postwar generation to do with all that?

A sensible young man, born right around the mid-century mark into the welcoming embrace of Oceanside, California, home to Phil Edwards and L.J. Richards, might go surfing. And play some Buddy Holly, Link Wray, psycho surf music while he was at it. Which is what Jim Evans did.

"It was really easy to crank up the reverb and hit a minor chord and you were there," laughs Evans. "I thought I was going to be a musician and not an artist."

We're sitting on the deck overlooking the front yard of his tastefully modern concrete-and-steel home. The garden is a drought-resistant ensemble of native plants and rocks. There's not a lot of fuel onsite for the fires that can consume whole swaths of Malibu at a time. Lessons learned.

The comfortable minimalism carries over to the interiors, which, for a guy whose artwork is known for its vibrant color palette, is subdued in blacks, browns and grays. Evans' office, adjacent to the deck, has the look and feel of an elaborate command-control station — with a daunting lineup of consoles, digital hardware, screens and wires. If there's a Matrix, it can be hacked from here. Evans gracefully lets his visitor pick up and strum the '62 Fender Jaguar propped against a north-facing wall, one of the visible nods to the age of analog.

As a kid, Evans demonstrated a proclivity for art, and by the time he was close to graduating high school, he had a few seminal moments under his belt. One occurred when he ran across a guy doing hand-brush sign painting at a local business. "I told him I'd work for free if he taught me how to do that," says Evans, tall and fit in his early 60s, and still wearing mostly black.

An apprenticeship began and Evans started learning brushstroke and script the old-fashioned way. He also learned that art could be both commodity and commerce when a high school teacher agreed to pass him provided Evans paint the sign for his surf shop.

"In the morning, I'd surf and in the afternoon, I'd paint his surf shop."

And in the evening he'd play in the bands for which he did the art, logos and promotional materials. Before long, other bands were paying Evans to draw out their personas. The relationships between art and identity started to take root in his consciousness.

But many other things were in there, too: the Bikini Atoll hydrogen-bomb detonations, the fallout of which literally poisoned the crew of a Japanese fishing boat and figuratively awakened the sleeping monster, Godzilla; the Korean War; the Cuban Missile Crisis; JFK's assassination; the first wave of friends coming back from Vietnam who "weren't the same guys anymore."

The utopian ideal of waves, of surf, and sun was still lingering in the atmosphere, but so was change, and it was moving fast.

"By '66, things had changed really, really fundamentally," says Evans. "The '60s opened up a floodgate of change that I can't say has happened before or since."

There was LSD, of course, and Evans had a common initiation. "Being an idiot, I didn't feel anything and took another [hit]. It was never the same after that."

Forays into Eastern Mysticism, the Tibetan Book of the Dead, followed. "There was this giant world I knew nothing about." Evans says his head became like a projector, taking in all that cultural dissonance and putting it down on paper in his drawings and cartoons.

"I thought I might [have been] retarded, or had ruined my brain," he laughs.

To stave off the draft, Evans enlisted in both the Naval Reserve and the Chouinard Art Institute, now known as CalArts.

"It was just a big free-for-all at that time," says Evans. "I just cartooned. I was basically a dopey cartoonist."

But dopey cartooning sometimes seemed like the perfect medium to make sense of the times. And doing comics for underground papers like the *L.A. Free Press* and then-counterculture mags such as *Surfer* connected Evans with seminal ZAP Comix artists like R. Crumb, Manuel "Spain" Rodriguez, Robert Williams and, most importantly, Rick Griffin.

***

Evans made lasting contributions to the genre, including the Yellow Dog series, which came out of Berkeley's legendary Print Mint, along with his own Dying Dolphin and, of course, Tales from the Tube, *Surfer*'s early '70s gonzo brainchild. Some of the work found him collaborating with Rick Griffin, who was also busy at the time helping to put the Haight-Ashbury ballroom scene on the map.

Meanwhile, Evans was soaking in the Venice Beach vibe. "It was a fertile time for art — late '60s Venice," says Evans. "There were a lot of great artists. I was in awe." When Griffin moved back to Los Angeles, he offloaded assignments to Evans. Before long, Evans was solidly in the mix. "I started getting so much work, I didn't even bother to finish art school," he says.

After an extended North Shore surfing safari that saw Evans testing himself at Sunset and Pipeline while creating iconic posters for Hal Jepsen's *A Sea for Yourself*, Bud Browne's *Going Surfin'* series and the instant Aussie classics *On Any Morning* and *A Winter's Tale*, Evans returned to the mainland in 1973.

Back home, he continued to trade in the most persuasive cultural currency of the day, doing album and logo work for the likes of Jan and Dean, the Beach Boys, Robby Krieger and Chicago.

Though the logos he designed for the Beach Boys and Chicago are still in use, arguably the biggest impact Evans made was with the Cadillac Wheels campaign, which both ignited and encapsulated the mid-'70s polyurethane-fueled skateboard revolution.

The campaigns were broad concepts, painted with a stunning attention to detail, contrast, movement and authenticity, all meant to communicate a paradigm shift. Evans cranked out one a month for five months, working with airbrush and dye, pencil for detail and toothbrush for texture.

For Evans it seemed like the creative universe was ever-expanding. "I felt really conscious of it," he says. "I thought it would move linearly."

Unfortunately, things slowed down right after the skate and punk explosion.

"The combination of Reagan and AIDS did a lot to bring things to a halt," says Evans. "I didn't know there were that many pissed-off people."

Evans devoted his energies to doing what a lot of people tried to do in the '80s — make money. "There was a point when I started to separate from Rick and those guys, and that was when I decided to feed my family," he says.

The '80s may not have been revolutionary, but they were remunerative. Evans expanded his poster work into Hollywood proper. Among his more lasting efforts were John Carpenter's

Dark Star and Neil Young's classic concert film *Rust Never Sleeps*, for which Evans did the posters, titles and animated opening sequence.

"He liked to get really stoned and talk a lot," says Evans of Young. "He had a lot of pop culture reference points. He was very specific."

Evans also marked this period with an increasing fine art output, teaming up with photographer Robert Knight to do prints of rock legends such as Stevie Ray Vaughan, Jimi Hendrix, Slash and more. Evans painted on layers of colors, added texture, patterns, symbols and distressed backgrounds to give the images an additional visual vocabulary that built upon Warhol's pop vernacular.

He called the work "icon narratives" and his limited-edition prints of Sinatra, Monroe, Madonna, Elvis and others found their way into some of the more high-end galleries of the day.

When the 1993 Malibu fire swept through Las Virgenes Canyon, the wood-framed California craftsman that used to be where Evans' concrete-and-steel house now sits "blew up as easily as it burned down."

"I didn't know how scary a fire looked or how fast it moved," Evans recalls. "There's a moment when everything goes silent and you know that everything you're going to have left is what's in your car."

When he returned after the fire, "the place was pretty much like the inside of a volcano." At one point, a horse walked into his driveway, bewildered and unclaimed. "It was surreal," says Evans.

Evans lost a great deal of his handcrafted archive. Even for a guy who has said he doesn't mind throwing everything in the fire and starting over, this was devastating. "I had PTSD for a while," he says. "I couldn't even look at fires."

A pre-fire encounter with members of L7 and Nirvana at a party turned out to play a big part in Evans' salvation. The bands asked him to do the first Rock for Choice concert poster, which he agreed to do. "And I liked it," he says.

***

That poster introduced him to a whole new generation of creative people who had grown up decoding the work of Evans and Griffin and their peers. At the same time, the energy coming from the early '90s indie music and DIY art scenes reminded him of the late '60s again.

"It was a really creative time and having been there before, I knew how it was going to play out," Evans says as we sit in his upstairs office, a sprawl of period-piece posters spread out on the carpeted floor. "It was almost like watching a movie of myself."

Under the moniker TAZ (Temporary Autonomous Zone, named after Hakim Bey's anarchist handbook) and in collaboration with his son, Gibran, and the master silkscreen artist Rolo Castillo, Evans cranked out more than 200 concert posters for the likes of the Smashing Pumpkins, Pearl Jam, Beastie Boys and Jane's Addiction and for iconic events such as Lollapalooza and the Tibetan Freedom Concerts.

"That was my therapy at the time. I felt fine because I could do anything I wanted. I'd do a 50-foot screaming Buddha and they didn't even question it," says Evans. "It brought me almost full circle to where I started."

But for Evans, back is only another way to the future. "He's kind of a future outrider, really ahead of the curve, and not terribly interested in being a part of it when it hits the mainstream," says Evans admirer and contemporary Craig Stecyk.

Which brings us to the NASA-like configuration in Evans' office. Encouraged, no doubt, by a lifetime of painstaking, hand-rendered work going up in flames, Evans became an early adopter of digital technology after the first Macs hit the mass market. "I couldn't see technology turning back from there," he says.

Evans moved into website development and viral marketing in the mid-'90s. He was undeterred by the millennial dot-com bust. "It was suddenly like they all thought dot-com wasn't going to happen. I thought that would be like thinking cars weren't going to happen in 1929."

Soon, Evans was developing websites for films such as *Men in Black*, *Seven*, *The Big Lebowski* and *Fear and Loathing in Las Vegas*. As creative director of Atomic Pop, one of the first exclusively online record labels, it was his job to figure out how to digitally infect people with the personas of Public Enemy, Ice-T, the Black-Eyed Peas and others.

"An MP3 suddenly makes a song not very sexy. You didn't have double-fold album covers anymore," says Evans. "I became known for doing viral campaigns."

Evans' current creative incarnation, Division 13 Design Group, does this on a massive scale. Working for just about every major studio, Division 13 has done the websites for the *Ring*, *Shrek*, *Saw* and *Ice Age* franchises and dozens more films from *Kung Fu Panda* to *Dreamgirls*.

These days, though, a movie website isn't just an online poster, it's a portal to the parallel world that the film signifies. Making those worlds engaging is something Evans calls the "simplicity of attacking the psyche."

Evans is content to attack the psyche from his command center in his concrete-and-steel bulwark tucked away in the Malibu Hills. Yes, he's working on a series of fine-art works that will apply many of the digital techniques to his iconic, hand-rendered images from the past, creating a whole new visual tableau of shape, color and reference. But until that's ready, he's in the Matrix.

"I find myself having interactions and collaborations with people on a huge scale and I never meet them. I'm okay with that, so I'm probably a good guy for the future," he says. "The real experiences are going down to Malibu and surfing with my buddies and hanging out and going to movies. Then, to come back here and have the world as your playground is actually fascinating . . . the computer is the collective unconscious that Jung actually talked about."

MAGIC AND LOSS

Originally published in Huck Magazine

"Deep inside the barrel, completely in tune with my inner self, nothing else matters, the hard wind and spit shooting past me from behind, my hand dragging along the wall, the light shines ahead." —Mathew Tomson, Becoming a Man, April 24, 2006

Sometimes, you slip into a seam where there's just enough of something to crack your shell and make you believe in things you might otherwise not.

On a summer afternoon in Montecito, just south of Santa Barbara, the shuttered cottages of the old Miramar by the Sea summon memories dating back to the turn of the twentieth century and the railroad barons and bootleggers who hid out there. Cross the tracks at the end of Eucalyptus Lane and a stone staircase leads down to a little cove. There, a woman sits staring out at the bay. Despite her reverie being interrupted, she graciously answers questions about tides and says it breaks here when the direction is just right and even sometimes when it's not. She tells of mysto swells that pop up out of nowhere, even in the summer, bringing in a wave that breaks across the entire cove. All the locals find their way into the lineup for a ride or two before the swell disappears again, she says.

Squinting in the direction she has pointed, you can almost see the waves trying to form. For a minute, it isn't hard to imagine a nice, head-high peeler coming off the point and Shaun Tomson locked into it, just ahead of the foam ball — legs wide, knees bent at a perfect 90 degrees, right hand stroking the wave, eyes fierce, following the light as he moves up and down the wall inside the tube like no one has done before.

I ask the lady if she knows Shaun Tomson. Of course, she says, everybody does. She says there's a path at the top of the stairs that takes you to the other side of the cove to Hammond's Beach. That's where Shaun can usually be found if the waves are breaking.

The beach lies at the end of a bougainvillea-framed lane, where a couple of families picnic in the dusk. When I bring up Tomson to a middle-aged woman having cheese and wine with her mother and best friend, she practically squeals. "He surfs here all the time," she says. "He's *sooo* handsome. And so nice, too."

Hammond's abuts a meadow that was once a burial ground for the indigenous Chumash tribe. The Chumash are gone, but a monument bears the inscription:

The Sacredness of the land lies in
the minds of its people. This land is dedicated
to the spirit and memory of the ancestors
and their children.

I will soon learn that the beach is special for reasons other than the Chumash and the long rights when it's breaking. This is where Tomson liked to hang out with his son Mathew. Here, one day, Mathew Tomson started picking up cobblestones and arranging them into a circle. Then, with his father's help, he grabbed more cobblestones and made another circle inside that circle. And one more inside of that. And inside that, two stones to sit on. Next, Mathew took a stick from a pile of driftwood and used kelp to attach feathers and brought the staff and his father into the center. This, he said, is the sacred story circle. In here, we pass the staff and tell stories.

Surfers are natural-born storytellers. Surfing is just a great way to get to the heart of the story, to find the arc that goes from darkness to light. Shaun Tomson knows this as well as anybody.

***

It's still dark the next day when Tomson pulls his black Audi station wagon into the Coast Village Inn at just past 5 a.m. The idea is to drive 20 minutes up the coast past Santa Barbara proper to Refugio Beach, one of Tomson's favorite spots. Tomson is tall and trim, and at 57, the pretty-boy face that became an icon of pro surfing's early days has been forged into something more rugged and soulful. The bright blue eyes that seemed to scorch perfect lines into whatever wave he rode are just as intent.

Santa Barbara is a long way from Durban, South Africa, where Tomson grew up in the postwar baby boom, the son of an Olympic-caliber swimmer and volunteer lifeguard at the Bay of Plenty. During the war, Ernie "Chony" Tomson served in the South African Air Force, a tail gunner in an American-made B-25 Marauder. Chony manned twin .50-caliber Browning machine guns in the fight against the sort of fascism that had scattered the Jewish Diaspora to far-flung places such as the Cape of Africa.

Growing up a beach rat with younger sister Tracy and older brother Paul, Tomson was kept blissfully naïve about his own country's brand of fascism. "When we grew up, we had an idyllic existence," he says. "We weren't really aware of the political aspects of our lives because that was the status quo when you were young and living across from the beach and surfing incredible waves. It was only when I started traveling that I realized I was living in an environment where great portions of the population were being repressed, subjugated and were the victims of unfair and unjust laws. But growing up, I had a wonderful life."

An international influence that did permeate the Tomson household was that of Hawaii, though the introduction to *aloha* was less than ideal. After the war, a 22-year-old Chony Tomson started training for the Empire and Olympic Games. Then, while bodysurfing with friends at South Beach near his home, he was attacked by a Zambezi (bull) shark that nearly ripped his arm off and almost killed him. Chony flew to San Francisco for extensive surgery and then to Hawaii to recover. Staying at the Royal Hawaiian Inn, Chony fell in with the Kahanamoku clan — legendary waterman and surfing's first international ambassador Duke Kahanamoku had been a childhood hero — and immersed himself in Hawaiian culture.

"My dad never had anything but a smile on his face," says Tomson. "My earliest memory is of my dad taking me by the hand into the water, teaching me how to swim. He used to say, 'Never turn your back on the ocean,' which is very profound. I think he meant you have to be aware at all times, but, also, don't give away what you love."

Despite his own setback, Tomson's father encouraged his son's growing interest in surfing. In 1969, when Shaun won the biggest local contest, the Gunston 500, Chony had a different bar mitzvah present in mind than the stock certificates his son's classmates received. He took Shaun to the North Shore of Hawaii. It just happened to be the famous winter of 1969, the winter of Greg Noll and the biggest wave ever ridden, a wave witnessed by only a handful and that has existed primarily as the stuff of oral history and legend.

"It was, like, the biggest winter ever in Hawaii," says Tomson, lighting up at the memory. "Makaha is where Greg Noll took that wave. We were staying in an apartment five floors up. We had the best views." Then, he casually drops a bomb: "I still have Super 8 footage of that wave, but I'll never release it . . . the legend is worth more."

We're back in town at Tomson's favorite breakfast joint after Refugio came up flat. Several locals hail Tomson as we stand in line, trading small talk and surf notes. Tomson greets each like a next-door neighbor, taking care to provide a brief bio, like a good host would. After ordering eggs and a side of fruit, he digs into the story of his first memorable foray into huge Makaha surf.

"I paddle out and it just keeps getting bigger, massive beyond belief," says Tomson, eyes wide. "Makaha is not like Waimea. At Waimea, it's one big takeoff and you do the bottom turn and you're out. At Makaha, the wave gets bigger and bigger and you're locked in, there's no way out. It's pretty scary."

As Tomson scratched his way into the lineup, legends Randy Rarick, Keith Paull and Rolf Aurness (son of James Arness, from *Gunsmoke*, and a great surfer) greeted his arrival with a chorus of, "Shaun, what the fuck are you doing out here?"

"I went, 'Uh oh,'" he says between bites, his still-thick South African accent making it feel like the story is being shared among mates at a barbecue. He managed a couple of waves before wiping out, "and it's like mountains coming. I just see mountains."

When a wave was about to crash on his head, Tomson made a rookie mistake and turtle-rolled under his board. "The wave held me down and I didn't think I could make it to the surface. I got up and the next wave hit me, and the next wave," he says, almost laughing. "That was the closest I've come to drowning."

Tomson went home a little shaken but plenty stoked. He started winning every local contest. After fulfilling his mandatory Army service, Tomson thought he would go to university and then into business. There was no such thing as professional surfing, just a handful of ragged contests here and there and Tomson had little left to prove at those.

But fate intervened at the 1974 Gunston 500 in the form of strapping Australian Ian Cairns, who convinced Tomson to join him and fellow Aussies Peter Townend, Mark Richards and Rabbit Bartholomew in Hawaii. That winter and the next, the leaders of the "free ride" generation created professional surfing as we know it: formally, by introducing the idea of a pro circuit with a world championship — the International Professional Surfing tour. More importantly, though, were the stylistic innovations they made in the proving grounds of the North Shore and Bonsai Pipeline, where Tomson and Richards in particular laid down the physical laws of modern surfing: attacking Pipeline backside; making deep drops into deeper barrels; carving inside the wall; flaunting power, speed and technical maneuvers in massive waves.

The revolution wasn't quite televised, but it has since been immortalized in surfing folklore, books and documentaries — most notable being *Bustin' Down the Door*, a film Tomson helped produce, which beautifully documents the creative chaos and culture clash that ensued. Things got heavy. Death threats were thrown around and the Hawaiian old guard meted out a painful dose of comeuppance to this new, transgressive crew. By the time reconciliation had been forged, the future of surfing had been written, and the professional circus — complete with sponsors, prize money, however small, and something like careers — started to take shape.

***

In his own way, Tomson helped catalyze how the industry would function. "I got my first free wetsuit from Pat O'Neill in November 1975 in Hawaii," he says. "It was a yellow vest and because I had a big year the wetsuit was featured on many magazine covers all over the world. I saw all the coverage so I wrote to Pat asking to be paid to wear the wetsuits. He agreed and

I became the first member of Team O'Neill, an idea Pat had been working on, inspired by the ski industry."

Tomson earned a reputation for power and fluidity in all conditions, but it was his tube riding that turned the world upside down and earned him a place in the top 10 of *Surfer* magazine's greatest surfers of all time. Before Tomson, Pipeline specialists such as Gerry Lopez would draw a straight line through the barrel and come out the other end as stoic and graceful as possible. Tomson, though, turned the tube into a canvas, a place to express himself in bold, powerful strokes.

"I felt like I could comprehend time better than anybody else," says Tomson. "Time would slow down. I could look at the wall and the curve of the wall and understand its complexities better. I had this innate sense of riding inside the tube. At times, I even felt like I could control the wave."

From there, draw the line to Tom Curren, Andy Irons and Kelly Slater, who himself has confessed awe at what Tomson did backside, single fin, at Pipeline. Tomson would go on to win the Pipeline Masters, Vans Triple Crown and 1977 World Championship and be named one of the 25 most influential surfers of the past century.

If Tomson has a light about him it's not because any retrograde, surf-god glamour illuminates him. He and his mates earned peanuts so the Slaters and Fannings could earn millions. They made something out of nothing and that something is now a $10 billion global industry. But Tomson's true measure came post–professional surfing, after the contest victories and adulation died down.

In 1990, when Tomson retired, there was no such thing as a lucrative endorsement deal for surfers put out to pasture. You had to make your own way. While still touring, he started Instinct surf wear, which did well enough but bottomed out in 1990. So, with newborn son Mathew in tow, Tomson and his wife Carla returned to their native South Africa where Tomson fulfilled a promise to his parents to complete his education — a 35-year-old undergrad at the University of Natal.

"I loved it," says Tomson. "South Africa was very rigorous academically to go to university. It was very much the Oxford-Etonian concept of building the Renaissance man."

Tomson and Carla returned to the States and started another line, Solitude, in 1998. It, too, had its ups and downs. At one point they were going bust, and had everything packed up on a Friday in preparation for a Monday shutdown. Only the phone stayed plugged in. "As long as the phone was in, there was hope," Tomson laughs.

That Sunday, a man approached the father of one of Mathew Tomson's Little League friends and asked where he could find the shirt the guy was wearing. The Little League dad said he'd better hurry, and passed on Tomson's number. Solitude was back in business on a handshake deal the next week. Tomson and his wife sold Solitude and Instinct to Oxford Industries, a large apparel company, in 2006.

***

Becoming a man is hard stuff. You're not born into it; you arrive at it through loss, struggle and determination. I've been lucky enough to meet some great men in my time — Muhammad Ali, Desmond Tutu, Ray Charles, my father — and the one thing they have in common is an indescribable presence. Shaun Tomson has that presence. Walking through town, at his barber's, wherever we go, people greet Tomson as if they want to take a piece of him home, put it in a vase and make a centerpiece out of it.

It should have been a good year, 2006. Tomson's businesses were finally settled. His son Mathew was going to his parents' native South Africa a generation after apartheid for a semester at Tomson's old prep school. And Shaun's book — *Surfer's Code: 12 Simple Lessons for Riding Through Life*, which spins surfing-based aphorisms such as "I will catch a wave every day" into beautiful parables — had just come out to good reviews and great sales.

Instead, though, it was the year things went dark; the year 15-year-old Mathew accidentally died playing "the choking game," wherein kids asphyxiate to get a brief high. Tomson didn't know when he wrote *Surfer's Code* that he'd need every one of its lessons about patience, courage, commitment and perseverance for himself.

A turning point came when he was by his wife's side in the hospital's psych ward. "I didn't think Carla was going to make it," he tells me. "She no longer had the will to live." A friend who had also lost his son came to visit. The friend had been working with a grief counselor, a swami. The friend said the swami had a message from Mathew. "It was a clear day," says Tomson, "a day like this. And a lightning bolt hit the hospital and the whole hospital shook — a completely clear, cloudless sky, and the message was, 'Mathew just wanted to tell you that he's sorry, he made a mistake.' You know, that gave us a connection with our boy," says Tomson.

Three years later, they adopted Luke. "*Adopted* is too weak of a word," Tomson told me on the drive up to Refugio that morning. "It's more like he chose us, like the universe put us together."

These days, a typical morning in the Tomson household begins with three-year-old Luke waking them up at 6 a.m. "He'll come rushing in, barreling into the room with us," says Tomson, admitting that it's his favorite part of the day. Then, Tomson will make Carla a latte and they'll all lie around in bed watching the news. Next, it's get Luke off to school and start working on one of the many projects they have going. "If the surf's good, I'll always try to get in a session," Tomson admits.

Tomson lives in Santa Barbara not because he got rich off of his apparel business — he didn't — but because he likes the vibe. He likes that the global environmental movement started here after the horrific 1969 oil spill: Tomson became the first professional surfer to join Surfrider Foundation in 1984. That's him doing the radical bottom turn on their T-shirts.

His Spanish-style home, a few blocks north of the Coast Village Road, is a relatively modest affair, considering the neighborhood. It's tastefully appointed — Tomson's wife, Carla, is a designer and it shows — and there's a large, inviting backyard. "I love the atmosphere up here and I love the people and the very laid-back lifestyle," he says. "It's not as frenetic."

We sit at a large, wooden table off the kitchen. The afternoon sun fills up the backyard behind us and a sturdy tree in the middle of it throws just enough shade. Carla offers coffee while Tomson shows me his latest project, a children's book called *Krazy Kreatures*. It's an A–Z illustrated encyclopedia of some of the more ominous sea creatures. It's done in verse and is quite charming; Tomson himself seems delighted by it. Another book, *Code*, a collection of useful affirmations aimed at kids, is slated for a 2015 release with the working tagline "Join the sacred story circle." For every copy purchased, a book will be donated to needy institutions.

Alongside his books, Tomson has incorporated elements of his experiences into motivational speeches for corporations, universities, elected officials and environmental groups. It all began when Glenn Hening, the founder of Surfrider Foundation, asked Tomson to give a speech inspiring the Rincon Homeowners Association to replace their septic tanks, which were leaking into the bay. Tomson went home and outlined what became *Surfer's Code* in 20 minutes.

Recently, Tomson addressed the Santa Barbara County board of supervisors. He titled his talk "The Light Shines Ahead." It began: *We all live in a challenging sea and our attitude towards those challenges defines who we are, and how we live our lives. Our attitude about the present defines our future. Our attitude about the future defines the present. Our attitude defines how we see the world and how the world sees us. Our attitude is the light that can show us the way on a journey from where we are, to where we want to be. It is a fundamental choice for all of us. Positive or negative. Optimism or pessimism. Hope or despair. Light or darkness . . . This is a story of a journey . . . a journey from heartbreak to happiness, a journey from the dark into the light.*

"You never know who needs what you can give," Tomson tells me. "You know, we got a gift from this woman who gave us life without asking one thing in return."

He tells the story of a black South African boy he helped put through school back when he was competing. They hadn't spoken in 20 years, but the boy, now a man, came to Mathew's funeral and he and Tomson reconnected afterward. The man had gone on to earn two degrees and become headmaster of a school teaching 1,300 kids. He asked Tomson to visit the school to speak.

"I went to his school. Impoverished. Impoverished. They didn't even have an assembly hall," says Tomson. "The headmaster came and [addressed] the kids before me. It was like Martin Luther King [Jr.]. These kids have nothing but their school uniforms and their blazers and skirts, and they're immaculate and you could see he had empowered these kids. Two of these kids spoke after I spoke — these kids could be at the head of the class at Princeton, Stanford, Harvard, Yale, Berkeley. What this guy has done is amazing."

As the day winds down, a kaleidoscope of colors dances in a soft sun, and a sea-misted breeze carries the smell of pink ladies and poppies. Tomson shares another story, about how just the other day Luke came into his office when he and Carla were looking at a picture of Mathew on Carla's computer screen, a black-and-white photograph.

"And Luke walks in and looks at the picture of Mathew and he says, 'Look at the rainbow.' It's a black-and-white picture," says Tomson. "On the day Mathew died, he spoke to Carla and said, 'Mommy, I'm standing under a rainbow. I'm in the perfect place.' So, you know, it just gives you the knowledge that our lives are brief, but there's this connectivity and sure, you know, it's terrible that we lost our beautiful boy and we can't hug him or kiss him, but his spirit is around us."

PRINCE + DARKNESS

Originally published in the LA Weekly

I'm deep into a harrowing Diane Sawyer special about hillbillies in Kentucky (a cautionary tale about the pre- and post-natal effects of Mountain Dew if ever there was one) on a cold and stormy night in early March, when something slams into my front door, causing me to jump off the couch.

Opening the door, I spy an anonymous brown package on the porch. Inside is the novel *Pain Killers*. It is signed *To my friend, Joe, Jew for a day —Jerry*. Armed with his fourth novel since his breakthrough book, the memoir *Permanent Midnight*, Jerry Stahl has, in his own inimitable fashion, done a drive-by.

Pain Killers continues the adventures of Manny Rupert, the hapless, hopelessly romantic (in his own damaged way) cop-cum-detective we got to know and love in *Plainclothes Naked*. This time a septuagenarian Jewish millionaire named Harry Zell, who wields his walker like a shillelagh, enlists Manny to go undercover as a drug counselor at San Quentin. Rupert's mission it to determine if a certain peroxide-blond 97-year-old inmate is in fact none other than the Nazi Angel of Death, Dr. Joseph Mengele. As if that isn't nettlesome enough for the illicit substance–susceptible sleuth, his first night on campus reveals his ex-wife and love of his life (who offed her first husband in *Plainclothes Naked* by serving him a bowl of Drano-and-glass-laced Lucky

Charms) has taken up with the leader of the prison's Aryan gang . . . who happens to be Jewish.

How's that for a setup?

Sitting there with his big, brazen new novel freshly hurtled into my living room, I got to thinking about Jerry Stahl and how, in a fashion that's so typically Los Angeles, it may be lost on some of us what a treasure we have in him. To his friends, he's a quick-witted curmudgeon who hides his bleeding humanity behind a gruff demeanor, black leather jacket and self-deprecating joke. To critics he's either "a better-than-Burroughs virtuoso," as *The New Yorker* once described him, or someone whose brash style, transgressive compulsions and unnerving thematic content is a source of visceral discomfort. He's been called the dark prince of literature, and his style has been dubbed gonzo noir.

But that's just lazy labeling. The truth is that Stahl brings a surprising empathy and a sharp social critic's eye to bear in his examinations of marginal characters and American dysfunction. Sitting with him at Vic's, he tells me about the inspiration for his latest.

"It came from the rage of living in a country where Bush was doing all this insane stuff in our name, and that somehow metastasized into writing about the link between America and the Nazis and how we were still killing people who were considered less valuable than us because they were nonwhite and in some way that folded into the Nazis and Mengele, and I married that into this obsession . . . It's that fact that this prison porn, *it's fascinating*," he says. "Everyone thinks [MSNBC] is Rachel Maddow and Matthews and Olbermann, but what it really is, is some guy named Pepe who's been in this shoe in Pelican Bay and is now on TV making gang signs."

How pop culture melds with the unseemly underbelly of our society is a topic ripe for thesis papers. It's hard to imagine anyone other than Stahl tackling such themes so starkly and so entertainingly at the same time. *Pain Killers* is both in your face and subtle at the same time. It's the work of a live-wire mind, one I've gotten to know and appreciate over the years.

As we sit for lunch — and at Jerry's request I'll spare the rote atmospherics, except to say that as princes of darkness go, Stahl is one handsome fella, who is quick to laugh and poke fun at himself — his book is just out in the world receiving the wild mix of raves and repulsion that accompanies a Jerry Stahl novel. I ask how's he's feeling about it all.

"There's no silence like the great roaring silence after a book comes out," he says. "Like, you write the book and the beautiful heartbreak begins. I'm just glad it came out, man."

They keep coming out. *Pain Killers* is his fourth novel in the past decade. There's also been *Love Without*, a celebrated 2007 collection of short stories (one of which, "Li'l Dickens," detailing a strange encounter with a not-so-closeted Dick Cheney, debuted in *LA Weekly*). He's prolific for any writer, even if he isn't also writing for film and television, on various essays and nonfiction and a hilarious blog called *Post-Young*, which looks at the world from the jaundiced eye of an aging hipster.

I wonder what keeps him so committed, especially considering writing novels these days can so often seem like an exercise in masochism or martyrdom.

"Well, if you don't have a book published until you're 40 . . ."

"You were 42," I correct.

"Okay, you know better than me. So much the better, so much the better," he laughs. "I write like a man being chased."

There's plenty of real-life reason for Stahl to feel this way. His father killed himself when he was young, and his mother has battled severe depression most of her life. His self-inflicted, near-death experiences are well-documented. And then, there are the exigencies of middle age.

"My best friend right now, my oldest friend from high school, is dying. I just went to say goodbye to him. He had a melanoma that metastasized and went to his brain," says Stahl. "It's very sobering when you reach that age when suddenly people you went to high school with, you know, your asshole buddies from way back when are . . . Everybody in my life has always died like *that!* [Snaps his fingers.] So this, somehow seeing all that is a motivation to either work really fast and do a lot or do nothing at all because of . . . what the fuck? I just write fast because I'm running . . . I have a real sense of mortality and the fact that I kinda shouldn't be here, you know?"

I first became aware of Stahl in the mid-'90s through a girlfriend who was rapt with his memoir, laughing and gasping in equal measures as she read. In the small-world department, turns out a dear friend happened to be his dear friend and suggested back then that I send a draft of a novel I was working on to Jerry. Why not? I thought, never expecting to hear anything back. Within two weeks I got an earnest and encouraging note back — the sort of thing that can keep an insecure novice going. Those who know Jerry are used to such acts of generosity. If he can help a writer get an agent, a book deal or a blurb, he will. He's also been known to host a Super Bowl party featuring copious amounts of Indian food and plenty of flatulent friends at his hilltop Mount Washington home.

More importantly, he's taught creative writing at Sylmar Juvenile Hall, a real-world incarnation of something that's obvious to anyone who's read his books. Stahl has a soft spot for the long shot. He's long been one himself. He grew up just a few miles and worlds away from where I did, outside of Pittsburgh. That's not the most nurturing place for a budding intellectual, and the town where Stahl grew up, Brookline, is the kind of place that is euphemistically called working-class. As a Jew in an oppressively Catholic 'hood, Stahl spent a good part of his childhood getting beat up for killing Christ. "I must have done it in a blackout," he jokes.

I ask how that experience informed his writing.

"It's just that no-bullshit town. It's not exactly like you feel any entitlement or superiority. I mean the word *jag-off* [one of Pittsburgh's finer contributions to the language] says it all," says Stahl. "It defines me because for many reasons I still feel like an outsider."

Like many writers, Stahl came upon his craft by process of elimination.

"It was more about the things I knew I didn't want to do. I would have loved to be a great rock and roll guitarist, but I kind of sucked. I just wanted a job that you could kind of do naked, fucked-up and alone at 3 a.m., and maybe get paid for," he says. "Reading guys like Nathanael West and all these guys who said shit I couldn't believe people were allowed to say, Terry Southern and all those guys . . . just did something for me. Writers are badasses to me. You know, Mailer, Pynchon, Tom Wolfe, Flannery O'Connor in her own weird way, they were just subversive individuals and that's what I wanted. I knew I was never going to be in the gainfully employed world. Put it that way."

After graduating from Columbia University, Stahl lived in New York City at the Columbus Circle YMCA, which at the time was a far cry from the polished YMCAs of today. He says he was "flailing miserably with some drug issues" while trying to scrabble together a living writing for publications such as *The Village Voice*, *New York Press* and *Penthouse*, for which he developed a knack for writing fake letters about zany erotic encounters.

"I was building up my résumé at *Beaver* and *Club International*, just to impress the NEA when I applied for those grants and didn't get them years down the road," he jokes. "Just scuffling."

But the talent for outré fiction was always there. An early short story he submitted to *Hustler* was rejected before going on to win a prestigious Pushcart Prize.

"It was for the Bicentennial. It was about a guy whose penis turned into George Washington's head. Highbrow. Couldn't be prouder of that one," he laughs. "I just wrote all the time and lived this deluded, drug-addled life in a five-floor walkup with a bathroom down the hall."

Stahl came to Los Angeles in the late '70s when *Hustler* publisher Larry Flynt moved operations out here after he was shot and paralyzed. The job didn't last long, but, as anyone who's read *Permanent Midnight* knows, he found some bittersweet success in writing for television shows such as *Thirtysomething*, *Moonlighting* and *Alf*. He also wrote six unpublished novels and went deeper into drug addiction before finally getting clean. His memoir rose out of desperation.

"It was really a function of survival. I was having a hard time writing. I hadn't written for a long time because of all the shit that is kind of associated with me and literally ran into someone on Hollywood Boulevard, Nancy Gottesman, who I'd known from *Los Angeles* magazine. I used to write a column for them . . . She said, 'What the fuck happened to you?' And, long story short, I ended up writing this thing called 'Naked Brunch' for *L.A. Style* and somehow an agent found it and after much shucking and jiving, I ended up getting a book deal."

I ask if he found it ironic that his first major publishing success turned out to be a memoir.

"Totally ironic. I had spent my life using words to hide the truth. My novels were never about me . . . The idea of exposing emotions, pain, heart, in a personal way, was not in my repertoire."

It is now. Underneath the wild satire and machine-gun-fire humor, Stahl's novels, especially *Pain Killers*, are full of the pain and pathos of characters confronting and often being overwhelmed by the indifference, at best, and cruelty, at worst, of life. Manny Rupert, for example, is struggling mightily despite his obvious personal disadvantages to adhere to his own ethics, mangled as they may be, in a country where complicity in such things as Mengele's research at the Nazi death camps reaches to the highest levels of polite society, and where TV networks turn the travesty of our prison system into entertainment for the masses.

In many regards we live in an Orwellian fever dream and we barely stop to ponder this, let alone skewer it the way Stahl does. "I don't know if they're going to put me in the same rack as Noam Chomsky, but in my mind, it's a political book," Stahl says.

As we finish our lunch, I tenuously suggest to Stahl that he's become a sort of éminence grise of L.A. letters, which, to me, signifies something far different and perhaps more interesting than it would in, say, New York.

"If that's the case, nobody's told me," he laughs. "I haven't seen the official notification of that, but thank you."

More importantly, he says, "I got this kind of second chance and I want to do something with it. And on another level, writing's easier than life."

DAVEY LATTER

Originally published in the LA Weekly

Davey Latter isn't moving to Silver Lake, not yet anyway. But he thinks about it all the time.

"I love Silver Lake. I love those mountains and I love those little houses with the yards. I would love to live there," he tells me over breakfast after we surf his favorite South Bay break, just north of the converted garage he's been living in for years in Hermosa. The dark-haired, ruggedly handsome and very tattooed Latter is picking at a bowl of oatmeal with a graceful modesty that almost mocks my assault on a plate of eggs, sausage, hash browns and pancakes.

"A bowl of oatmeal?" I ask. "What the fuck's wrong with you?" After all, Latter is the erstwhile drummer of the almost-famous Stanford Prison Experiment, a mid-'90s hardcore, confrontational band in the vein of the slightly more famous Jesus Lizard.

"Did you see me flying around on the water out there? I got 12 waves to your one," he needles. "Now go ahead and eat those hash browns and pancakes."

It's true, he was flying around out there. I love to watch Latter surf. A couple of times, as I was paddling back out after a meager ride, I had the pleasure of being in just the right spot to see him cut back on a wave and turn down its face into the next section, pulling rabbits out of a hat on a less-than-epic day. If I had a camera, I'd get a cover. At 43, he's still one of the best, if not *the* best, out there: fluid, fast, always in rhythm.

Latter taught me how to surf several years ago when I signed up for a class. He took more of an interest than was necessary, going so far as to help me pick out the right equipment and then bring me down to San Onofre, a gentle wave that does wonders for the confidence of a newbie. He didn't have to, but he's like that.

It'd make sense for him to move to Silver Lake, though. More and more that's where his scene is, and where his friends are. He plays drums in Great Northern and Everest. Before that he played in Earlimart, Slidell, Fairuza Balk's band ("She's a great musician") and Fireball Ministry, most of which are in the Silver Lake scene.

He's lived in Los Angeles before, back when SPE was on the verge, making records and touring and causing a bit of a stir.

"We all lived in the same house in L.A. and practiced five times a week and that's probably why we had the little success we did have," he says, "because we were super into it. I want to do that again and that's why I was almost getting ready to move up there."

Besides, the beach isn't what it used to be. A bunch of nouveau-riche types started moving in about 10 years ago and have just about wrecked the place. Made it hard for guys like him to survive.

"It's horrible. I was born and raised here and I love it. I should have *Hermosa Beach* tattooed across my back. But now it's like . . . " he trails off, no need to explain. "For a while it was great. The girls were beautiful and the waves were great. It was awesome."

***

Latter stayed in Hermosa after his mom took his four older siblings up north to Redding to escape some chaos in her life. He was 14 at the time.

"She had a major drinking problem," he says. "But my mom was rad. She raised all five of us."

Raised him right too. Latter stayed in school even after she was gone and he was crashing on older surfers' couches. While his friends were cutting classes to catch waves, he set attendance records. Still has the certificates.

Latter's dad had left the picture years before. "I came along and he split. He played pool. He was a hustler and a womanizer. He died about 12 years ago."

Latter and his brother took his ashes out to sea and let him go.

I ask him if he felt safe, being on his own so young.

"It was pretty hectic," he says. "I think it was the surfing that kept me here. I was a total surf kid."

As a teenager he tore up the junior circuit, winning contests up and down the coast, getting sponsorships, traveling. And then something happened. "I got my heart broken," he says. "That, literally, was the end of my surfing career. I got my heart broke really, really bad and I couldn't get out of my first heat of the day."

He turned to playing the drums, for therapy really. Not surprising since he came of age in the heyday of the Hermosa Beach punk scene that spawned bands like the Circle Jerks, Pennywise, the Descendents. "I live on the street where Black Flag used to practice," he says.

Since then, it's been a never-ending string of day jobs and near misses. Still, he's survived, which isn't nothing. Some of the people he grew up with haven't been so lucky.

"A lot of them are dead," Latter says. "A ton of them are in jail."

And he surfs, just about every day. "It's a great way to start the day," he says, smiling. "It gets your body moving and it puts me in a good mood."

That helps when you're constantly broke, and Latter's constantly broke. Despite that, he's one of the most generous people I know. Generous enough to come out to my car and listen to a tape of my songs and act like my fantasy of him playing in my fantasy band, Middle-Aged Bastard, isn't such a bad idea. Generous enough to take a kook like me out to surf the best sandbar on the beach, where no one questions my presence because I'm with him.

His new bands are really good. I heard Great Northern on the radio the other day and the song was lush and beautiful. Latter thinks the main songwriter, Solon Bixler, is a genius, "the John Lennon of our era." He's stoked about Everest, too, a band comprised of Silver Lake all-stars from other bands like the Watson Twins and Earlimart and Alaska. Both bands have record deals with indie labels. He's hoping this is it, this is how he will finally be able to not sweat the rent and "have my breakfast paid for." But he can't help but feel the sands running through the hourglass.

"It's very scary. I keep saying this is my last hurrah in the whole music scene. I'm not 23 and it's a crapshoot."

Still, he's not moving to Silver Lake. Not just yet.

"I would love to live there, but I know I'd get in my car every morning and drive back down here," he says. "The salt water,!it!kind!of!sucks!me!back."

DYLAN, FOREVER

Originally published in the Los Angeles Times

My phone buzzed at 5:07 a.m. Monday morning with a text from a friend who was in India with his wife and son. The text read: "As Luke Perry goes, so does the world."

I was too groggy from the sleeping pill I'd taken to respond, but I remember registering awareness that Luke Perry was sick. Then again, I could have been dreaming. It wouldn't have been the first time Perry had visited me in my sleep.

In fact, there was a period when my life amounted to little more than brief and fraught interruptions between episodes of *Beverly Hills, 90210*. It was circa 1997-98 and the FX Network was playing four repeats a day of *90210* in sequence — at 10 a.m. and 11 a.m. and then at 4 p.m. and 5 p.m. On Wednesdays, when new episodes aired on Fox, I'd consume five hours of the show. Between episodes, I'd do the things I needed to do to stay alive — get coffee, take a walk, try to earn a buck as a writer — but watching *Beverly Hills, 90210* was what gave structure and purpose to my days.

I watched the show so much that when I tried to sleep, the theme song — a weirdly anthemic mash of hair-band, whammy-bar guitar and Kenny G saxophone — would ring in my head. When I did sleep, it was often merely a portal into the lives and dramas of Dylan McKay (Perry), Brandon and Brenda Walsh (Jason Priestley, Shannen Doherty), Kelly Taylor (Jennie Garth) and the rest of the gang. Even my dreams were episodes of *Beverly Hills, 90210*. At that rate of immersion, the lines quickly blurred between where the show ended and I began.

I was in my early 30s at the time, newly sober and living in a threadbare Hollywood apartment with a mattress on the floor and a cardboard box draped with a bandanna over it for a table. Like a lot of fools, I'd been propelled to this juncture by inchoate yearning. Maybe for some sunshine, maybe for a swim in the ocean, maybe for the fantasy of having grown up surfing Point Dume, driving a vintage Porsche and dating Kelly Taylor.

When I finally arrived in L.A., from a rented house in the Pittsburgh suburb where my family had landed after moving nine times by the time I was 10 — cities, states, countries — I'd moved 19 times in 32 years. By yearning, I think I really mean wanting a home.

Depression is a vortex and a vacuum. It sucks us in and we fill it up with obsessions. Sometimes our obsessions become our lifelines. Fred Exley had Frank Gifford and the New York Giants through which to live vicariously as an all-American football hero when he wrote *A Fan's Notes*. I had Dylan McKay and the Peach Pit, which suspended me in an amniotic California dream.

A little before 7 a.m., and still not fully aware of the gravity of Perry's situation, I responded to my friend in India: "Right?"

We were speaking in code at this point, signifying that we'd agreed we weren't ready to surrender Luke Perry to the final outcome yet. His fate might not have mattered as much 10, even five, years ago when mortality for our generation, Generation X, was more abstract. But the death of singer Chris Cornell a couple of years ago seemed to signal a change. A recent Centers for Disease Control and Prevention report shows mortality rates for Gen X are on the rise, fueled by suicide, alcohol-related diseases and economic downturns.

If that wasn't bad enough, Gen X was nowhere to be seen when CBS recently posted a list of generations — from the silent

(1928 to 1945) to the post-millennial (1997 to now), wiping us out completely. Squeezed by a media fixated on boomers and millennials, maybe we really are the Lost Generation — and maybe rallying around Perry is a way of being heard. Then again, most of my cohorts reacted on social media to the CBS snub in typical Gen X fashion: "Whatever, never mind."

It's hard, though, to overstate what a sensation Luke Perry was back in the day. He was beautiful enough to cause commotions in tabloids and in teenagers' chests, but there was always more to Perry than a pinup. He seemed strong and decent. His eyes were full of mischief and kindness, and he said a lot with a little. In an era that's bestowed tech disrupters, investment bros and chattering-class screamers with some sort of exalted holy status, Perry had the whiff of a more sacred American archetype about him. Maybe we were just proud of him.

When I posted something about Perry's death on social media and mentioned how surprisingly deeply he'd gotten under my skin, I half expected to be made fun of. This was, after all, Dylan from *Beverly Hills, 90210*.

Instead, the thread filled with similar sentiments. One friend wrote about how Perry had offered to help her pick up dog poop on Park Avenue when she was struggling to handle two Great Danes. A writer friend who interviewed him a few years back shared that she had saved a sweet voicemail on her phone for a long time: "Hey, Em, it's Luke Perry." A third friend said he was kind to a childhood friend of hers, who was just another Hollywood studio minion at the time. "Let's just say he didn't treat her like a minion," she wrote. "He knew her name and would pop in and say hello."

And even though *90210* could hardly be called prestige television, the show was good. Maybe not five-times-a-day good, but it didn't last 10 years because it sucked. Something about it salved my wounds from decades of dislocation, of always having one foot out the door, of being embarrassed by my sublimated vulnerability and desire to connect, of struggling with the harsh light of sobriety. Or, maybe they were old wounds from high school, where my résumé tells one story and my graduation pictures tell a different one about a kid with hair that never conceived of Dylan McKay's daring James Dean pompadour, whose right eye had a patch over it to conceal that it was green, black and swollen shut and whose hand was in a cast — a pirate costume on someone who was desperate to be normal.

Dylan wouldn't have tried so hard. He had his own code and he rarely got ruffled. Even on TV he was more authentic than me.

Sure, the Peach Pit crew had their struggles. They fractured and wounded each other, but they helped each other heal too. They knew one another's scars. I was surprised to find myself in my early 30s longing for that intimacy.

Often aloof and mercurial, Dylan nonetheless was the gravitational force in their universe, almost like a father. He took in the rubes from the Midwest and sheltered them with his cool. His affirmation enabled gawky David Silver to come into his own and annoying Steve Sanders to find some grace. Dylan was respectful to women.

I'm not ashamed to say that in the early 1990s when I was in my late 20s, I grew out my sideburns and tried to do something with my hair. I remember walking down a street in San Francisco one night with a couple of female friends. We were, or at least I was, inebriated. Three men passed us on the sidewalk, one of them muttering something incredibly rude at one of the girls under his breath. I stopped and asked him, "What the . . . did you just say?"

He taunted back, "Oh, who are you supposed to be, Dylan McKay?"

I took off my prized, brown leather jacket, tossed it to one of my friends and calmly walked back toward them, my intentions clear. "Yep," I said.

Under Dylan's dominion, the Peach Pit crew became worth spending time with — a lot of time, in my case. We heal in our sleep, and I don't sleep much or very well. I think what I was actually doing with all the *90210* viewing was surrogate sleeping. I was trying to heal.

Perry left the show in 1995, seeking more significant roles. Things didn't quite pan out, and he returned in 1998, just as the funk I'd been in started to lift. I didn't tune in as much after that, but I remained thankful for all that Perry had given me when I needed him. I agreed he deserved better material; we both did at that point. I tried to do something about it when I found myself driving to Texas with Wes Anderson on the eve of *Rushmore*'s release. We were somewhere in Arizona, I think, when I suggested an inspired casting-against-type of the sort that would garner rave reviews and launch a sublime second act à la Bill Murray.

"How can you miscast him?" Anderson asked me.

"I suppose as a bus conductor or an airplane pilot."

"He'd just become that," Anderson replied. "He's such a chameleon."

Anderson was probably half a decade too young to get it. But Quentin Tarantino, born a few months after me, understood. Perry's final film appearance will be alongside Leonardo DiCaprio and Brad Pitt in *Once Upon a Time in Hollywood*.

At 10:21 a.m. my friend texts me again: "Dead . . . wow."

I come clean with him about my decades-old *Beverly Hills, 90210* obsession. He hits me right back. "He was underrated. I mean that."

All that time and I wasn't really alone.

PART THREE

Burdens and Privileges

"One is meant to last forever,
the other is meant to last six months."

THE CONFIRMATION OF DANNY KWOCK

Originally published in The Surfer's Journal

Danny Kwock's hair is long. Like, hippie long. This might surprise those who've leafed through the tome *The Eighties at Echo Beach,* or are old enough to have been there and remember when Kwock, Preston Murray, Jeff Parker, Peter Schroff and their Newport Beach confederates upended surfing's no-fun ethos with a blast of punk-rock style and attitude.

Kwock's long hair has gray streaks in it, but not enough to betray his 56 years. Not much does. He is slim and sinewy, and he wears bracelets and rings and necklaces and appears to be unafraid of turquoise. The bearing is a little more Native American than new wave, but save for the crow's feet and frown lines, he still reads a lot like the dervish who helped turn the stretch of sand between 54th and 56th Streets into the so-called "hottest 100 yards."

When I approach the front door of Kwock's wet-sand house on Miramar Beach, the guy who helped rocket Quiksilver and the entire surf industry into its orbital trajectory (before it all came crashing down a decade ago) is on the back deck staring past the point toward Hammond's reef. This is one of the Santa Barbara retreats where Kwock has spent the past 12 years in peace negotiations with himself, trying to make friends with the quiet.

He seems slightly startled when I rap on the door, but warmly invites me into his bright living room. Kwock's beach pad is minimalist: a couple of couches against the walls, a coffee table in between — nothing to distract from the real show out the window. Two things do, however, command the interior. One is the '61 Martin acoustic propped up against the wall. I quickly learn the guitar sounds as smooth as Tennessee whiskey cut with a drop of honey. The other eye-grabber is a framed Woody Woodworth photo, circa 1977, above the couch.

The shot is of Kwock making a crazy drop at the Wedge, while enforcer Ron "Romo" Romanosky perches comfortably on the shoulder. Kwock came across the pic when he and one of his four sons noticed a display with a polka dot surfboard, and some familiar looking trunks, at the Newport Beach Surfing Museum.

"My son goes, 'Whoa, Dad, they did, like, a shrine to you.' And I was like, 'Really?' I didn't even know. And then I was like, 'Oh, yeah, that's one of my old boards.' My son looked at the photo and goes, 'Dad, that's you. Your name's on it.'"

Kwock says he doesn't collect many pictures of himself, but this was a must-have. "There are so many stories in this photo. There's Romo and all my buddies that became legendary bodysurfers — Terry Wade, 'Mel' Thoman — all these guys that were in the *Dirty Old Wedge* documentary. They're all right there, you know?"

Not to mention the shorts he's wearing.

"Those are one of the pairs of shorts me and Preston Murray, my buddy, got caught stealing at Quiksilver, which was how I got my whole career," he laughs. "I'm wearing one of them right there."

A creation myth in 35 mm.

***

The shot was taken during the "Bustin' Down the Door" days, when South Africans like Shaun Tomson and Aussies such as Ian Cairns, Rabbit Bartholomew, and Peter Townend were lighting up the North Shore while wearing an exotic brand of trunks that actually stayed on in consequential surf — and didn't look like dishtowels. Kwock and Murray just had to have a pair.

Before their infamous caper could even be possible, though, Jeff Hakman and Bob McKnight had to meet while surfing in Bali/Hawaii (accounts vary). The pair bonded over how they both wanted to turn their passion for surfing into a sustainable enterprise. With OP and Hang Ten gone to the malls, and Birdwell Britches getting long in the tooth, they struck on the idea of acquiring the American license for Quiksilver boardshorts. A considerable amount of hazing by Aussie founder Alan Green ensued, including a gonzo weekend in Las Vegas, but soon enough McKnight and "Mr. Sunset" were living together on the top floor of a house on 59th Street while sewing and snipping at a Quonset hut on 17th Street in Costa Mesa.

The work situation made Newport Beach their go-to surf spot, but they mostly stayed away from what was not yet known as the hottest 100 yards. Kwock and his unruly crew, however, did not go unnoticed.

"He and his co-brats would hang out at 54th and 56th Street," laughs McKnight. "I'd see him flying around and yelling at people and taking more than his share of waves and I was like, *who is this little shit?*"

Soon word got out to the little shits that hard-to-find Quiksilver shorts were now miraculously at hand. There was just one problem.

"Quiksilver was like 25 bucks, you know? It was like Air Jordans, and we were broke," says Kwock. "I was like, 'I'm okay. I'll wear my old OPs.'"

Preston Murray had other ideas. They decided to "borrow" his mom's Chevy Vega while she was playing tennis. The newly permitted Kwock was tapped to drive them up to the Quonset hut in Costa Mesa.

With Kwock piloting the old beater and Pink Floyd on the 8-track, they made the short drive. Kwock parked in the lot, and Murray crept into the back of the tin shack. A couple minutes later, Murray came running out with a large stack of shorts in his arms, yelling for Kwock to open the trunk.

"I said, 'No fucking way, dude! Take that shit back, we're going to jail, that's too many,'" says Kwock. "He goes, 'Shut up!' and just throws it in the back and slams the door and says, 'Let's go, dude!'"

Murray had grabbed a stack of size 36s — about eight inches too large for the teenagers — so they went around to the local shops trying to trade them in, claiming their grandparents had bought them the wrong sizes.

"He had this whole freaking story, you know," says Kwock. "He's such a mastermind."

Eventually, the scam filtered back to McKnight and Hakman. Meanwhile, a jealous kid on their surf team ratted them out. "We were kind of showing off at school," says Kwock. "So, he freaking narc'd on us."

The two were summoned to face the music. Murray, who came from a well-off family, could mostly buy himself out of the predicament. Kwock had to work it off at the warehouse. There was something else, too.

"I told him," says McKnight, "that part of his penance was, when he saw me and Hakman, or any of us out in the water, his job was to paddle 100 yards away from us in any direction, or go in. That was one of our rules."

Playing against type, Kwock showed up to work, kept his mouth shut and did his job.

"We got to know him and like him," says McKnight. "He was a good worker."

***

Long before he was a notorious boardshort bandit, Kwock was just "a kid from the 'hood in Kalihi," whose mother tried to keep him away from the waves. Of Okinawan and Dutch descent, Kwock's mom had grown up surfing and told stories of carrying big redwood logs on her head. But, the beach life was also full of cautionary tales.

"She had this fear that I was going to be a beach boy," says Kwock. "She'd say, 'Those guys, man, they live that life, but they can't make money and support their families.' I was always more pushed into sports. I did Little League and all that stuff."

Kwock's dad was a one-time professional bowler and full-time hustler, who left a complicated legacy, genetic and otherwise. He had three children with his first wife, four with Kwock's mother, and "a couple we just found out about on the side," says Kwock. The tree is twisted enough for Kwock to have a nephew older than he is.

The elder Kwock was a bit of a dandy who inherited some land and money, and was also an ace chef. Under his dad's guidance, Kwock's aunt Helen opened up Helena's Hawaiian Food, a longtime Honolulu icon and recent James Beard Award winner.

According to Kwock, his father's club, Dan's Den — "this smoky lounge with these singers who would go on and play jazz and stuff" — was one of the first places to give Don Ho a break. As the story goes, Don's uncle hit up Kwock's dad to give "the Hawaiian Perry Como" a slot on stage.

"My dad said, 'We're getting out of that slow stuff. We're going into rock and roll, but I'll give him an off night,'" says Kwock. "So, he put Don Ho on the off night and I guess someone saw him and he got discovered."

Though he tells this story fondly, Kwock is less sanguine when he talks of how his father could never quite get off the booze, the hustle, the cigarettes and the women.

"He freaking lost everything, man, because of his alcoholism and his lifestyle choices," says Kwock. "Next thing you know, my mom's just trying to hang on for dear life and raise us. They crashed and divorced, and that's when we moved to California."

Kwock already had his first taste of surfing by then, though it came courtesy of *Five Summer Stories*, not mushy Waikiki waves.

"I remember watching it on the big screen at Kaimuki because it was a big deal for surf movies to come to town," he says. "When I saw freaking Gerry Lopez at Pipe and heard the music from Honk, it was like a light went on. It was just insane. What I saw was a creative dance and art form in this organic setting in nature. The water was our paradise in Hawaii."

After the movie, Kwock ran to the store and bought a *Surfing Magazine*. He started putting pictures up on his walls. One in particular captured his imagination.

"I remember this one shot. There was this guy — he was in California, which intrigued me, because he had a wetsuit on. It was this long wall and he's taking off and he's falling and it looks scary and it looks exciting to me. And I looked at it and read the caption and it said, 'He who hesitates is lost.' I used to look at that every day."

***

California was less intriguing in real life than it was in that photo. It was farther from the water, too. Or, at least, the San Fernando Valley was, where Kwock's mother moved Danny, his sisters, and his stepdad in the early '70s. Kwock went from *Five Summer Stories* to Valley smog and Catholic school.

"It was a shocker to me. Next thing I know, I'm at this Catholic school having to wear covered shoes and a collared shirt and tuck it in. I remember getting racked by the nuns with rulers."

The culture shock was too much for Kwock's mom and stepdad, and they "just got in the car and started driving south," says Kwock. The idea was to keep going until the smog wasn't visible. A wrong turn off Interstate 405 put them on the road to Newport Beach. They stopped when they ran out of peninsula. "They couldn't drive anymore, so they were like, 'Let's look for rentals here.'"

The house was right in front of the Wedge, though at the time that had no significance to Kwock, who'd been left behind in the Valley to finish up junior high at Catholic school.

"I was just all by myself, living with my aunt who's an opera singing teacher. It was kind of creepy, lonely vibes," he says.

His parents eventually retrieved him, but Kwock's first day of school in Newport almost made him wish he were back in the Valley.

"I'm the minority guy, not the majority. I'm sitting there and kids are teasing me, calling me names, calling me out," he says.

The day ended with Kwock delivering a Hawaiian-style beatdown to one of his tormenters. He was sent to the principal's office, but ditched instead and started hitching home, where he got royally chewed out upon arrival.

"I'm like, 'I'm fucking over California. Fucking *haoles* are mean. I want to go back to Hawaii.'"

Kwock was so unruly, his mom ended up giving him his wish, and sent him to live with an aunt in Ala Moana. He says he went feral that summer, catching buses to Sandy Beach, hitching around the island, staying away for days at a time.

"I was an adult going into eighth grade," says Kwock. "My aunt couldn't handle it." Before she could bounce him back to the mainland, though, Kwock started stand-up surfing at Waikiki and Portlock Point.

"It clicks, right? I'm in Hawaii and I'm like, 'Yes, this is the land of surfing . . . and, oh, my God, *I love surfing.*"

Back in Newport, feeling rudderless and unwanted, surfing became a way for Kwock to forge an identity and garner some much-needed affirmation. The jetty-formed rebound wave that occasionally broke outside his front door would be his crucible.

On big days, the "nasty beast," as Kwock calls the Wedge, pops up like a snarling monster and breaks furiously into a shallow, cement-like sandy bottom. Ten people have died surfing there since they started keeping tabs, and dozens more have been paralyzed. Back in the mid-'70s, it just wasn't stand-up surfed. And, anyone willing to take his chances would have to run the gauntlet of grizzled watermen — bodysurfers and knee-boarders — led by Romanosky.

"They didn't let anybody surf there," Kwock says.

The old guard, though, took a liking to the lost boy and allowed him into the lineup.

"The dudes down there were very affirming to me as a little kid, because I was different, you know? Hawaiian kid, ethnic kid, and into what they were doing. I was a bodysurfer first, skim boarder . . . I did what they did. I loved it. They knew that I liked surfing so they let me do my recreational craft, because they liked me. I was always watching them with eyes curious to learn how to be a man, because I had no father figure."

After taking countless beatings, Kwock finally made the drop.

"I was the only one standing up, trying to be Gerry Lopez," Kwock says. "I was trying to be Gerry Lopez at the Wedge. That was kind of my deal."

***

Back then, Quiksilver was a bottle looking for lightning. McKnight and Hakman had the best boardshorts in the business, but they didn't have a business to go with their boardshorts. They needed to build the brand.

Meanwhile, Kwock and the Echo Beach kids had started turning up in the surf mags almost as much as the pros on tour. McKnight and Hakman realized that their inmate might hold the keys to the kingdom. When Kwock finally finished working off his debt, McKnight set up an audition at 56th Street.

It couldn't have come at a better time for Kwock, who found himself caught again in the grip of something familiar and inchoate at the same time.

"I wasn't living in Hawaii anymore. I was pissed off at my teachers. My mom and [step]dad were melting down. I was living at friends' houses a lot. I just wanted to be a pro surfer. I was angry."

Kwock acted out at the Wedge, suffering broken bones and near drownings in his determination to master the wave. Once, he was knocked unconscious in shallow water, resulting in "a bullet hole" in his head from a fin, and a subsequent police escort to Hoag Hospital.

Another time, he found himself pinned to the bottom under "a million pounds" of water after taking off on a huge wave.

"I felt my fingertips on the sand like *whoosh*, like they were feathers and everything was super slow and all of a sudden I started getting these visuals of me on the bottom. I remember saying, 'Okay, you can't lay down here forever, it's super comfortable and it feels really amazing, *but you gotta push up.*'"

It was during this period, when "life seemed the worst ever" for Kwock, that McKnight approached him about coming on board.

"All of a sudden, these guys are saying, 'Hey, we want to make you a surf star. We'll get you your dream of being a pro surfer.'"

They set up a few photo shoots for Kwock and it was all starting to click, except for one thing.

"I'm looking at the Quiksilver shorts I'm wearing, [and thinking] *these are so freaking ugly and boring.* They're like this brown, beige, muted color, old floral prints that aren't happening anymore."

Kwock pleaded with Quiksilver to "make more radical stuff," but they weren't having it. Instead, they told Kwock to concentrate on getting pictures in the magazines and entering contests. He had other ideas.

"I remember my girlfriend at the time would wear these super cute dolphin shorts. They were new wave, and I'm like, 'I'm gonna rock these out surfing.' I put them on and I freaking go out with all the photographers there and sure enough, I get my first big picture in *Surfing Mag.*"

In the aftermath, Kwock was called to the carpet again. McKnight wanted to know why his sponsored rider was getting snapped wearing red-and-white striped shorts. "I was like, 'Dude, look at my board. *It's got polka dots on it!* And you're making me wear these brown, old, hippie shorts — with that? That era is over. New wave and punk are the new deal.'"

After some resistance, the bosses gave in and put together a line featuring stripes, checkers, diamonds and polka dots.

"They put them on the rack and boom, they went like hotcakes," says Kwock.

Soon Gotcha followed suit and, suddenly, the boating and polo-shirt capital of the West Coast was one of the coolest places on earth. "Echo Beach started the whole thing," says Kwock.

"That shot in the mag was like the first shot with those kinds of graphics. And then Preston started putting checkers on his board and polka dots, and Parker started putting stars and then, Alan [Green] saw it and was like, 'I get it.'"

McKnight and Hakman may have thrown Kwock a lifeline when he desperately needed one, but he gave them something back they needed almost as badly.

"He saved us from being some old-guy thing," says McKnight. "He was listening to the Clash and we were listening to the Rolling Stones. He knew the market like an edgy kid and we followed that into surfing. He's very responsible for making Quiksilver a cool, connected thing."

Of course, it wouldn't have worked if Kwock and company couldn't back it up in the water.

"Danny was a really good surfer," says McKnight. "He was insane, doing all those modern moves, power surfing with an edge. Whenever Newport was big, he shined. People didn't necessarily like him for it, but he was legit."

Bill Porter, reminiscing in *Newport Magazine*, captures just how radical a figure Kwock cut at the Wedge: "I remember it like it was yesterday. His shortboard had primary-colored polka dots and a Quiksilver logo. And sure enough, he made the drop. I'd never seen anything like it. [He] not only surfed the Wedge, he shredded it. I've witnessed spectacular feats in major sports, but nothing compares to this triple-overhead tube ride capped with an off-the-lip snapback. Danny won't remember that particular wave like I do, because for the next 90 minutes, he continued to tear into the Wedge in ways I didn't think were possible."

***

There was no such thing as a surf industry in 1976, and it's not too much of a stretch to say the multibillion-dollar lifestyle and cultural signifier we know today sprouted from the sands of Echo Beach. Riding that zeitgeist, with Kwock as team rider and then team manager and then a company Jack-of-all-trades, Quiksilver shot to $20 million in sales by 1986. McKnight, a USC business school grad, then took the company public.

A few years later, Kwock signed 18-year-old Kelly Slater to an unprecedented contract. "When he told me he got him, and what he paid him, I almost fired him," laughs McKnight. He could afford to laugh: Quiksilver's sales had hit $100 million by 1990.

What comes after $100 million? For a while, it didn't seem like there was any ceiling. After signing Slater, Kwock and McKight launched Roxy, the first women's surf label. Roxy rolled out its own show, *Surf Girls*, on MTV. It would grow to be a half-billion-dollar brand at its peak.

By the mid-'90s, Quiksilver had become something like surfing's rock and roll circus. Kwock was equal parts ringmaster and rainmaker — the guy who had to be at every party and lasso every star. His Hawaiian roots and street cred were critical to luring iconic bad boys such as Johnny-Boy Gomes, Derek Ho, Sunny Garcia and, later, the Irons brothers into the fold. He signed Slater, Machado, Beschen, Irons, Lisa Anderson — some of whom left for other brands, eventually, while others remained with Quik for decades. Zeitgeist impresarios such as Preston Murray, Richard "Wooly" Woolcott, Steve Jones, Peter Schroff and others followed Kwock to Quiksilver. Companies like Gotcha, Stüssy, Volcom and Hurley rose up within a 20-mile radius.

Kwock, though, was starting to feel the grind. He'd gotten married in 1987 to the daughter of a wealthy Newport developer and had four kids at home. He was away a lot and when he wasn't away, he wasn't really there. Drugs had become part of daily life, work and otherwise.

"I'm just burning out, but things are getting bigger and the company is getting more corporate. In the beginning, I was super excited. I remember McKnight was more stressed. I was more reckless. I'd be like, 'Dude, let's go for it. Let's be like Levi's on the beach. Let's be the first billion-dollar company in the surf industry and give surfers jobs all over the world!' I was just into helping surfers. I think that was probably from the cocaine, just me being crazy."

In the midst of this, the receptionist at Quiksilver called Kwock to let him know that "a little old man with a cane and a

Bible" was in the lobby asking for "Danny Boy." Kwock's father used to call him Danny Boy when he was a kid. "I didn't like it because he'd sing that song all drunk and it just used to bug me."

It had been many years since Kwock had seen his father. He'd heard he was in an old folks' home somewhere. He wasn't sure. Now his dad was in the lobby of the company where Kwock had a big office and a portfolio of responsibilities — marketing, media, brand development, acquisitions, entertainment — which was expanding as quickly as Quiksilver was. He had one request.

"I don't want to die in California. I want to die in Hawaii," the elder Kwock told his son. He asked if Danny would fly him back home. Kwock bought his dad a one-way ticket and drove him to the airport. On the way, Kwock told him about his wife and kids and his life. "We bonded, and buried the hatchet and made amends," says Kwock.

His father died a few years later.

At the time, Kwock was at the annual Quiksilver meeting in Tavarua.

***

Grow, meet quarterly projections, exceed shareholder expectations. "Finance, budget, spreadsheets, gross margins, fucking Wall Street," as Kwock puts it. This wasn't punk rock — this was big business. Not to mention all the damn entertaining. "Twenty-four-fucking-seven entertaining," says Kwock.

The pressure and the partying were starting to get to him. One rainy night on the North Shore, Kwock found himself out with some of da boyz, speeding down a wet road, long after midnight, hell-bent for a dive bar in Mokuleia.

"We're flying down the highway," he says, "100 miles per hour, and I'm like, 'I'm gonna die in this car tonight. This is not your everyday job prerequisite. This is going to go till three or four in the morning.'"

It didn't help that the team back at the office was also riding him about business-side details.

"So, I'm just beating myself up and I'm going, 'What the fuck can I do for you guys, man?'" Kwock says. "'I can't do any more. I gave it all for you. I'm fucking living in the battlefield on the front lines in Hawaii, dealing with everybody and every fucking facet of this crazy-ass, billion-dollar business. And you guys are fucking giving me shit?'"

Few businesses have tried to square the circle of being cool and being a business like the surf business. It can work for a while, but eventually either the cool or the enterprise cracks.

"People that were businessmen were kooks when I was a kid," says Kwock. "I felt like I was pulling it off and then I said to myself, 'No, dude, I'm living a lie because I'm a corporate asshole. I'm becoming the person that I just dread being.'"

Back at the Quiksilver compound that night, Kwock lost it. "I remember just cracking and I broke down in tears. I got in the car and said, 'Fuck it, I quit, I'm fucking over it.'"

He hung on long enough for Quiksilver to blow by the $2 billion mark on its way to a peak of $2.5 billion in revenues — more than a quarter of the surf industry's business. When he did leave, it was under a bit of a cloud. A small investment he made in friend and former employee Richard Woolcott's start-up paid out handsomely when Volcom went public in 2005. Kwock was politely shown the door, which he was on his way out of anyway. He cashed out his stock and fled to Santa Barbara.

"I needed to be alone," he says. "I was around so many people. I was just tired."

For Steve Jones, the influential designer whom Kwock hired in 1985, something essential went missing in Kwock's absence.

"It wasn't until after he left that I really got it. Danny was the soul of Quiksilver," says Jones. "His rapport with everyone was the glue that spiritually held the company together. When he left, it was like the soul of the company walked out the front door."

***

In Santa Barbara, Kwock found himself suddenly quiet and extremely uncomfortable, even amid the many comforts his success had provided.

Ensconced in a converted barn on the Ranch, he would sit and watch waves form, break and peter out practically at his doorstep. He wouldn't move for them, couldn't for some reason. The newfound quiet felt just as heavy as those million pounds of water on top of him at the Wedge.

"I'd be at the Ranch watching perfect waves and I'd just start crying. There were times in the past when I had to get every wave in the lineup. Now I was like, 'I don't even want to go surfing.' I was saying, 'Man, I'm in trouble.' Everyone's thinking, 'Dude, you got the best. You got all the money in the world. You don't have to work. You got all this shit and your success, you've accomplished so much.' And I'm thinking, 'I'm a fucking douche. I'm a fucking lost child.'"

Suddenly there were no emails, no calls, no noise — no distractions. "You have a lot of time to think, and you have a lot of time to ponder, a lot of time to check in with your truths. Or you can choose not to do that and just get high. I didn't want to get high. I wanted to heal."

Kwock and his wife set up a foundation and started giving "many, many millions" to charities. He joined a men's therapy group, volunteered to do yard work and helped with art and music classes at his kids' schools. Still, there were times when the silence seemed like it might consume him.

He started going to church, where he met a priest named Father O'Donnell. "He doesn't remind me of what I think of as a Catholic priest. He just reminds me of my dad, when my dad was at his sweetest moments. This little Irish man, and he's so rad and he's got a twinkle in his eye," says Kwock. "He was fully into the Beatles, and we'd sing 'Let It Be' and he just pulled on my heartstrings."

Kwock chose to be baptized. "It was therapy. I remember praying about my life and what defines me, who I was and what I'd done, the wild ride I'd been on and why I wasn't happy for my successes. I just started praying and it gave me peace."

He'd sometimes see himself as a kid, staring at the Wedge, unable to resist its call. And he began to understand who that kid was and what drove him.

"That abandonment issue was there," says Kwock. "I remember, because at the Wedge, when I'd take off — *he who hesitates is lost.* 'Don't hesitate man. And I'm not afraid of dying. Fuck, if I die, good! I don't even want to fucking be here.' That was my attitude as a kid. I was kind of crazy suicidal, but that craziness got me fame. It medicated me. All those things started coming out of me later, as a man. I had sadness from when I was a kid, from being abandoned. That was where the real issues were."

Kwock's first marriage didn't survive the fallout. He recently remarried, however, to a woman who has two kids of her own. Now, he's the patriarch of a brood ranging from 14 to 28.

His attempts to parent the children for whom he acted "more as a big brother than a father" are awkward, but appreciated, says his son Ben, now 26 and the head of operations for *What Youth* magazine.

"He had his struggles," says Ben. "I don't see why he wouldn't, considering his broken family."

Far removed from the roar of the Wedge, the action of Echo Beach and the hustle of Quiksilver, Kwock lives in a tentative détente with his second act.

"I get up, feed my dogs, take them for a walk. My wife and I do yoga, or work out together, or hike or ride a bike. We'll walk on the beach sometimes. We just sit and talk and share moments. Having a blended family with six boys, that's enough for us to always be talking about their lives, all their stuff and what's happening. Then, a lot of times, I meditate in the morning and pray, and then do that again at night. I just live a slow life," he says.

Still, Kwock can't help but flash back to the past every now and then.

"It wasn't the money," he says. "I wanted to change the world. I wanted to blow fucking minds. It's that simple. Who in the surf industry today wants to blow fucking minds?"

Kwock recently closed on a house in Newport.

"He says to me and my brothers that this is a trial run," explains Ben. "But I can tell he's excited."

GOLDSTEINLAND

Originally published in Treats

In a glass-framed photo on a glass desk in a glass-and-concrete house high on a hill is pictured a fit young man with shoulder-length, shaggy hair. The man is resplendently dressed in a white, high-collared long-sleeve shirt, crisp, white slacks and black dress boots — a dandy in waiting, it would seem. The man in the photograph is years — maybe decades — away from his unlikely notoriety, but he already looks famous, like the DNA of a young Paul Simon and Doors-era Val Kilmer somehow collided. In his hand is a leash attached to an equally turned-out Afghan hound. The dog is important, once the love of his life, the man has said. And it was for that dog that this whole thing started.

Another photo catches the eye. The man is naked and bears a resemblance to a young, sun-bronzed Iggy Pop had Iggy decided he didn't like to sweat. In the picture he is flanked by two topless young women straight out of a California dream of sunshine and free love. Their knees meet above his groin and they smile like the fetching muses they once no doubt were. He stares hungrily at the camera, as if this was serious business. Maybe it was. There have always been fumes of rumors of flings with starlets and dalliances with lonely aristocratic women and mysterious heiresses but Goldstein will only let the pictures do the talking. "That's me and Jayne Mansfield at the opening of the Whisky a Go Go in 1964," he says casually. (One such rumor has Mansfield's husband at the time sending a few goons to break young Jimmy's legs.) You see, even though James Goldstein is a self-proclaimed "man-about-the-world," traveling over 300 days of the year — to fashion shows, basketball games, exotic hotels in equally exotic lands — and has hosted some of the more legendary Hollywood parties at his house, no one really knows much about the man. And, it seems, he's found the perfect persona: to be everywhere and nowhere at the same time.

There are plenty more photos on display like trophies. Here he is with Spike Lee, Penelope Cruz, Sean Combs, Snoop Dogg, Rihanna, Gisele, Cindy Crawford, Jean Paul Gaultier, Kate Moss, John Galliano . . . In these, he doesn't look like he did in the earlier photos. Eyebrow-raising haute couture, often crafted from exotic animal skins, has replaced the understated class on display in the photo with the dog. The hunger in the photo with the nubiles is gone, too. Now, he is ripened by sun and age and by being able to have what he wants. The photos are no longer documents of becoming, but evidence of having become.

***

I meet the man in the photos, James Goldstein, on a brilliant, sun-kissed spring morning at his home on a hillside in Benedict Canyon, Beverly Hills. I would come up again weeks later and the sky was equally crystalline, the air breezy, the view pristine. One wonders if the weather is always perfect up here?

Goldstein greets me in a cap, running gear and running shoes, all featuring fluorescent, lime-green highlights. He is small and wiry with a deep tan and long, wispy white hair spilling down from his python-skin cowboy hat; he moves with the air of an alligator in the sun and his words are so carefully chosen that you wonder if they are being meticulously carved, like stone and concrete, in his mind first. His voice is a low, guttural baritone that never loses its monotone rhythm. The house where we meet, his house, is one of modernist John Lautner's remarkable mid-century Los Angeles residences. It, along with the Chemosphere in Hollywood, Silvertop/Reiner Residence in Silver Lake, the Elrod Residence in Palm Springs, the Garcia House on Mulholland, have become symbolic of a certain sort of Los Angeles dream, be it design or lifestyle or both, which is, of course, as Lautner intended. And the Silver Screen has come a-calling to shoot in these modernistic, almost cave-like structures — namely as dwellings of villains.

Goldstein's home, known as the Sheats/Goldstein house has been featured in *The Big Lebowski* and *Charlie's Angels: Full Throttle*, among many others. Angelina Jolie got semi-naked here for Timothy Hutton in *Playing God*. It has been speculated that Lautner's stunningly bold creations attract Hollywood villains because they form perfect repositories for projecting limbic system overreach — flying too close to the sun, as it were. Or, to put it another way, since Hollywood traffics in mostly a puritanical moralism, despite its reputation, anything this good has to be bad. Goldstein, though, is no villain, especially when it comes to stewardship of Lautner's legacy. He resurrected this remarkable house and, to some degree, Lautner himself. Thanks to Goldstein's loving attention, this house is now part of the permanent record of aspirational L.A. architecture.

That Goldstein and Lautner would find each other could seem fated if you believed in that kind of stuff. Both grew up idiosyncratic independents in the conservative Midwest and both fell under the spell of Frank Lloyd Wright. Goldstein, the son of a Racine, Wisconsin, department store owner, discovered his passions at an early age. A friend who lived a block away lived in a Frank Lloyd Wright. His father's store was near the Johnson Wax plant, also designed by Wright. Thus began his appreciation of finer architecture, the modernist Wright buildings standing out from the typically drab constructions in Milwaukee and Chicago.

"Growing up, I was definitely focused on modern design,"

says Goldstein. "I was always looking at new buildings."

We're sitting on the pool's concrete deck, the sun is strong, the sky clear and the deck angles out above the horizon toward Century City, where Goldstein made some of his considerable, though somewhat mysterious, fortune. "Real estate investments" is all he'll say on the subject.

Those early impressions lasted as Goldstein made his way out west as a young adult. "As I moved out here and started traveling to Europe and being exposed to more and more varieties of architecture, I developed an appreciation for old designs that I never had as a boy, but at the same time I wanted to have something thrusting into the future, rather than something from the past."

I ask Goldstein if there was something in the optimism of Southern California's embrace of mid-century American modernism that made him want to break from the past, and especially the Gothic Midwest where a 13-year-old Jewish boy who liked to dress in pink suits might seek reinvention in the wide-open West. Goldstein reflexively dismisses the psychobabble, but hints around its margins anyway.

"Nah, I don't think that was the case," he says. "I like the clean, minimal look together with the feeling of the future and something that had never been done before," he says. "I liked the idea of creating something new and I liked the feel of openness, of bringing the outside to the inside. All of those things."

***

Helen and Paul Sheats commissioned the Sheats/Goldstein House, as it's known in architectural circles, in 1961. The couple had worked with John Lautner before in 1948 and 1949 on the L'Horizon Apartments in Westwood. The L'Horizon Apartments, with their space-age curves and dramatic angles, can be seen as a modest banner-raising for Lautner, who strives to set himself apart from the more formalist Frank Lloyd Wright protégés who preceded him here — Rudolph Schindler and Richard Neutra. Those two, perhaps more celebrated modernists, stayed mostly true to the egalitarian/socialist ontology of modernism (an aesthetic that would take decades to become the stuff of bourgeois desire), while Lautner was a little bit rock and roll — a maverick even within the progressive Frank Lloyd Wright school.

Lautner was born in 1911 in Marquette, Michigan, to an academic father and artist mother. Lautner's parents were art and architecture enthusiasts and key influences on Lautner. The Lautner family built their summer home on Lake Superior themselves. Lautner's mother designed and painted all the interior details — a formative experience for Lautner, who in later years would pay as much attention to the interiors of his homes as the exteriors. Lautner studied philosophy, ethics, literature, drafting and architecture along the way to earning a bachelor's degree in liberal arts at Northern Michigan University, where his father taught.

Though his parents were both fans of architecture and building, Lautner had little interest in the formal aspects of drafting and preferred, even during his fellowship at Frank Lloyd Wright's Taliesin studios in Wisconsin and Arizona, to stay out of the drafting room and get his hands dirty in the construction process, something he learned to love building that summer home.

Lautner came to Los Angeles, like Schindler and Neutra before him, to supervise various Frank Lloyd Wright commissions. He built his first solo project, the Lautner House, on Micheltorena in Silver Lake in 1939, a year after his arrival. It was an auspicious beginning, featured in a big splashy spread in *Home Beautiful* magazine and praised as the best house in the United States by an architect under 30 by the eminent architectural historian Henry-Russell Hitchcock.

It didn't take long for Lautner to showcase his derring-do. In the mid-to-late '40s the iconic coffeehouse aesthetic known as

Googie architecture was born, taking its name from the Lautner-designed Googie's Coffee Shop on Sunset and Crescent Heights, which followed the three Coffee Dan's restaurants he designed. The style — with its signature cantilevered structures, boomerang shapes, upward tilting rooftops, acute angles and high-energy scripts — became synonymous with the atomic-age kitsch that was often derided as too lowbrow and vernacular to be taken seriously by the architectural establishment. More recently, though, a critical reassessment has recognized Googie's value as an expression of sunny postwar populism and a worthwhile emblem of the times. No doubt, nostalgia has played a big part in that reassessment. But, the playfulness of the style, the optimism and the eye-catching forms would all become integral elements of Lautner's palette.

While Googie made a lasting impression on the commercial landscape of Southern California during its postwar coming of age, Lautner set about in earnest putting his stamp on the area's residential aesthetic in the mid-'50s, beginning with Silvertop in 1956. Then the Chemosphere followed in 1960, the Sheats (Goldstein) Residence in 1960 and the Elrod House in Palm Springs in 1968.

Lautner integrated the boldness of Googie design with the unique challenges each home presented. The Chemosphere was an answer to the "insane" (as he called it) practice of digging into steep hillsides to build foundations and structures. The Elrod House perfectly fits into the rugged desert bluff on which it is built. Silvertop looks as natural on the hilltop overlooking Silver Lake Reservoir as a cherry looks on top of a sundae. Surrounded by gauche neo-classical mansions rising up like warts in the foliage above Beverly Hills, the Sheats/Goldstein House is as unobtrusive as a cave in the side of a mountain. That Lautner manages this integration with the flair and style that set him apart from his contemporaries is testament to his particular genius.

***

Goldstein alighted from Milwaukee at 18 to go to Stanford. There he studied math and physics, but decided he wanted to get into finance and came to Los Angeles for grad school. Another problem with staying in the Bay Area: it had no professional basketball team at the time. Though he was yet to become, in the words of NBA commissioner David Stern, "the single biggest and most extravagantly dressed NBA fan in the world," basketball was still a passion, going back to his teenage days as a statistician for the Milwaukee Hawks.

"At that time," Goldstein says of his arrival in Los Angeles, "I was still involved with football and baseball, as a spectator, but I realized as the years went on that those sports didn't provide the same excitement for me as basketball. So, I decided I would specialize in basketball and dropped out of these sports and now basketball is almost a year-round occupation for me. Even in the summertime, I go to summer-league basketball and I go to international-league basketball. It got to the point where something I never anticipated happened and I became very famous as a result of my basketball involvement. And now I know almost everyone involved in the game — owners, players, management, ball boys."

I caught Goldstein on a rare day off from this hobby. Sitting near the opalescent pool, with shadows dancing on the water, he tells me he's been to 19 games in the past 19 days and the reason he is sitting here with me now is simply because there are no playoff games on this day. If Goldstein isn't jetting off to a playoff game, he might be heading to fashion week in Paris, Moscow or Milan, sitting, of course, in the front row at the catwalks as his leggy model "friends" gallop the runway in front of him. He speaks proudly of his "enormous" hat collection, many made from rare reptile skins — cobra, python, anaconda — purchased from a mysterious hat maker on a small, serpentine street somewhere in Paris. "I buy all my hats from him now," Goldstein says, like the gentleman is in the CIA protection program. "He's a great hat maker and I only wear his hats these days, which means I have a lot of other great hats that I bought years ago that never leave the closet."

He learned to love clothes from his father, but says at a young age he began moving beyond his father's conservative dress to his own creative style. When pink became a fashionable color in his teen years, he went all the way and dressed in all-pink suits. In his early 20s, Goldstein made a trip to Paris and was bitten by a lifelong fashion bug. Goldstein's business card says FASHION, ARCHITECTURE and BASKETBALL on it, and it might be hard to determine which of those pursuits he's spent more time and money on.

Goldstein's early years were spent living in various apartments in West Los Angeles. But, then came Natasha, the Afghan hound and love of his life. The dog needed room to roam. So Goldstein went house shopping.

***

The Sheats' residence had gone through several owners before Goldstein came upon it. In each case, the owners had insufficient funds to realize Lautner's design. Substandard materials — plaster, Formica — were employed to fill in the gaps. Goldstein found wall-to-wall green shag carpet throughout the house, the poured-concrete structures, including the triangle-patterned living room ceiling, was painted in black, white and green, the bedroom done in turquoise. It was like the '70s gone wild.

"It was a mess," says Goldstein, "but I could see the brilliance of the design."

The house, as with all of Lautner's residences, was designed to accommodate, not compete with, its environment. Built into a sandstone ledge high up in Benedict Canyon, the main structure spreads out at a 45-degree angle from the eastern rise. The entrance on the northern end, set against a dramatic jungle-like hillside, opens into a den, kitchen, dining area and living room with cement banquettes for seating and a beautiful cement, wood-burning fireplace where the northwest angles meet. The living room opens to a pool surrounded by a cantilevered, pebble-concrete deck that juts out into the horizon toward the Santa Monica Bay. It has to be one of the greatest man caves ever conceived.

James Goldstein bought the Sheats House in 1972, 10 years into its existence, for $182,000. "I know, it sounds kind of shocking," he admits.

Prior to buying the house, Goldstein spoke with Lautner on the phone.

"He expressed his pride in the house and strongly recommended that I buy it, but he hadn't been over to see what had been done to it until roughly 1979 when I brought him over — his mouth fell open."

Lautner had originally conceived of the living room being open to the pool area with an air curtain protecting the "inside." In other words, no obstructions, not even glass, to the outdoor environment. That never came to pass. Instead, previous owners had put in glass windows intersected by horizontal and vertical steel mullions. It was the exact opposite of the intent. Goldstein's first project with Lautner was to remove the mullions and replace them with frameless glass. Lautner was all for it.

"That was the first construction project I'd ever been involved with in my life and the first thing I had done to this house," Goldstein remembers. "Once I got my feet wet with that project, I was off and running with more things that I wanted to have done."

Goldstein and Lautner spent 15 years together trying to "perfect" the house. "We hit it off and I could see that we liked the same things and we both had a rebellious streak and didn't like conformity or the corporate mentality," says Goldstein.

I ask if it was the beginning of a happy ménage à trois, between him, Lautner and the house.

"It wasn't just the love of the house, it was the way our minds worked," Goldstein replies, ignoring the quip. "He was always very receptive to my ideas and what I wanted to do to improve the house. At the same time, he never imposed anything, or told me 'This is what I'd like to have done,' sometimes to the point of frustration because I would have liked to have heard his ideas."

Goldstein pauses. He looks around for a bit and continues.

"He always waited for my ideas and took them and enhanced them. He would typically come up with several alternative sketches for any of my ideas and allow me to pick the ones I liked the most and then we would do a small model of it and then we would do some actual mock-ups and then we would start the construction of it. At each phase of that development, we'd be making modifications as we went along, including the final construction phase."

He pauses again as if he is replaying the action in his head.

"There would always be modifications to try to make everything as perfect as possible without any regards to what it would cost. There was never a budget; there was never an estimate. It was always, how can we make this as perfect as possible without any regard to the cost."

Talk about a dream client. Architecture is a tough racket and even Frank Lloyd Wright was constantly struggling with money. Goldstein, with his sweeping program of first setting right, and then advancing, the designs must have felt like a godsend to Lautner in his sunset years.

I ask Goldstein, who estimates he's put $10 million into the project so far, if he had a big picture in mind or if the property evolved incrementally.

Long pause.

"I have to say, I didn't see a big picture," he says. "Maybe at some point later on I did, but I started out working incrementally and eventually I replaced the glass in the house with frameless glass, for example. Then, I just worked on every room of the house to try to achieve perfection. When I pretty much completed the revisions to the house, I still continued to work on little details."

***

Goldstein takes me on a tour. One that he must have done hundreds of times — from Lautnerites to movie stars to international architecture buffs to drunk party guests looking for an adventure. He moves slowly, making sure no anecdote is left out, and no matter what magical or beautiful thing he points out he never breaks from his nonplussed demeanor. The attention to detail is astounding. There is so much to take in, it's almost overwhelming. He points out the skylights on the roof overhanging the pool deck, which were filled in with drinking glasses by previous owners to save money.

"That turned out to be a great idea," he says.

The original pool had a waterline beneath the coping, surrounded by Mexican tile. Goldstein replaced the tile with concrete, per the original design, and raised the water level to affect an infinity pool. He added a planter on the west side.

The pebble concrete in the living area, which was covered with green shag carpet, Goldstein tore up and replaced the concrete bit by bit. The fireplace was made of rocks and Goldstein replaced it with concrete to match the building's poured-in-concrete structures.

Goldstein put in a two-level koi pond with a waterfall and concrete stepping-stones. The Lautner-designed banquettes are about the only thing that stayed as is inside. Retractable skylights were added. Goldstein fingers some controls and in a minute the sky is just a ladder as we stand in the kitchen. Other details: the main table-bookcase running along the east side of the house is a beautiful concrete-and-wood piece, done by Lautner and Goldstein, that used to be Formica -and-plaster cabinetry. A glass-and-concrete dining table that seats eight was designed and installed, a kitchen bar added. It's safe to say, given Lautner's affinity for interiors and the minimal opportunities to get his hands on them, the two enjoyed themselves.

As we move around the house, Goldstein straightens out picture frames, wipes countertops clean. Everything is so precise and immaculately maintained, one might hazard to think it's to the point of near compulsion. Dozens of bookcases are stuffed with books on travel, fashion, architecture and basketball. Magazines, from all eras, form perfect skyscrapers that dot each room.

A fun feature of the house is that you have to exit the primary living space to get to the guest bedrooms and the master suite. This forces you outside along the moat-like concrete decks and into the incredible environment Goldstein has submerged his house into. Indeed, the ambient sound of running water from the waterfall reinforces the feeling that somehow, you're inside a sort of submarine surrounded by a sea of green. That, too, is by design — Goldstein's.

The only time Lautner and Goldstein had a difference of opinion happened to be over the landscaping. Goldstein fell in love with tropical places when he "escaped" Wisconsin and wanted to move in that direction. Lautner preferred to plant pine trees. "He didn't oppose me, but I could see he didn't understand it either," says Goldstein.

I would have to say Goldstein got it right. He bought up the surrounding acres ascending down the hill to the street below and began planting tropical plants. "And that was the start of an immense landscaping project that has been continuing on for 20 years," he continues, as we descend concrete steps to his bedroom. "The hillside is apparently perfectly situated because the sun moves directly onto it," he tells me. "My landscape architect, who specializes in tropical vegetation, is amazed himself at the way some things thrive here."

We take a detour along one of the stone pathways and come to a deck jutting out into the thick forest. It has a glass bottom and peering down into it gives one the sense of looking into a kelp garden through a glass-bottom boat. As weird as it sounds, given that we're high up in the hills, the entire environment has the feel of looking into an aquarium or being submerged in an underwater observatory.

"It didn't start out as an ecosystem, but I think it ended up that way," says Goldstein.

We go down to the master bedroom. It features a pie-shaped leather couch with two raised, pie-shaped glass end tables on either side. The couch points out toward the northwest, an ideal spot from which to watch the sunset or the fog roll in. Windows above the bed offer a view into the pool.

Goldstein stops to adjust some books and pictures that only he would notice were out of place and apologizes for the mess, explaining that he's been away for a while. He opens the closet next to the bed and pushes some buttons and racks of clothes start marching past us on a rotating wardrobe.

"Here's the closet that probably houses one of the great men's collections in the world because I buy very special pieces," he says. Anyone who has tuned into a Lakers game and wondered who is the silver-haired gent in the green and purple and red snakeskin suits would have to agree.

Goldstein tells me his favorite designers are John Galliano and Roberto Cavalli. "Every season, I buy a new collection of clothes, and this most recent season my favorite pieces are from Balmain. I've found that men's clothes are very boring at the moment. Balmain makes some amazing jackets for women that have no real sexual connotation of any kind because they are motorcycle jackets. I've bought a couple of them."

While his clothes collection is flamboyant and flashy, and a Lautner house is almost flashy by definition because of the bold designs, Goldstein's taste when it comes to the property is pretty refined. Even the large sculptures on the grounds, one of wood, the other concrete, are masterfully integrated into the space. I ask him about the dichotomy.

"One is meant to last forever, the other is meant to last six months," he quips.

We descend farther into the man-made jungle, Goldstein bounding about like a mountain goat, me panting to keep up. Everywhere there are diversions — pathways leading to vistas of either the inner space he's created or the outer space that surrounds it — the city, the basin, the sky, the sea, appearing for seconds, then vanishing as you snake through more canopies.

Then, as if from a Disney movie, the trees part and give way to an open area in which is nestled the Goldstein Skyspace, also known as "Above Horizon." The structure was intended to be an arranged marriage between renowned light and space artist James Turrell and Lautner.

"I saw James Turrell's work in museums and also at the Pace Gallery [in New York] and I was really excited about it," explains Goldstein. "I was thinking, and this probably goes back to 1990, that I wanted a collaboration between Lautner and Turrell, the three of us had a couple of meetings and things were underway but getting the city to approve this was a laborious process. It took a number of years, and by the time I was ready to start construction, Lautner was no longer around. So, then it became a project with me and Duncan Nicholson [Lautner protégé and Goldstein's architect since Lautner's death in 1994] and Turrell."

Turrell provided the specs and dimensions for the room and Goldstein and Nicholson did the rest. It's an astonishing, almost Gehry-ish structure, jutting out from the green forest into the eternal blue sky. Goldstein had the idea to add a window in the southeast corner, "which Turrell went for and it turned out to be a great addition." The effect is something like looking through a porthole and catching a glimpse of the great sea outside.

Goldstein fumbles with a remote control that looks like something that would operate a Wii console, and a section of roof peels back to reveal the blue sky.

"That show starts at 7:30 tonight," he says. "It's not a sunset you see, but you see the changing colors of the sky. The sky doesn't look like the sky. It looks like the ceiling of the room."

I ask if he ever meditates here.

"I'm not sure what that means," he replies dryly. "I enjoy the experience no matter how many times I'm here. I'm not sure if you call that meditation."

***

Goldstein finished the Skyspace six years ago and turned his attention to his current major project, a multi-use facility on an adjacent property that will sit beneath a tennis court. The space will host a theater complex, nightclub, large bar, massive DJ booth, guesthouse, kitchen and surrounding deck/dining area. The structure will be bigger than his primary living space.

"I like the idea of separating my house with all the personal possessions from where the parties will be," he says.

I ask Goldstein, given his obvious flair for style, if he ever thought of getting into fashion or design as more than a hobby.

"People say that all the time — you should be an architect or you should have your own clothing line, but, number one, my tastes are too extreme to be popular from a commercial standpoint, and number two, I don't want to get burdened with the business at this point."

It's a little cliché to say, but it feels a bit like an Eden up here, although, perhaps, an isolated one. But it's certainly splendid isolation if it is that. I ask Goldstein how he ever leaves. "I love traveling, so now I'm only here five or six months a year." I suggest he could rent the forthcoming guesthouse to me for $800 a month. He laughs.

Goldstein tells me he's dropped out of the L.A. social scene recently and doesn't entertain as much as he used to, something he hopes to take up again when the new facility is complete. He doesn't know exactly when it will all be done, but guesses it could be up to five years. "They're supposed to pour the concrete on the tennis court this summer," he says, a bit skeptically. When I suggest he may kick the bucket before this is all complete, he chuckles and says, "Yeah, but what can you do about that?"

I can't help but wonder if Goldstein ever wanted someone to share this all with. He's never been married and he says he never really wanted to be.

"I need to be free," he says. "I don't like the concept of marriage — the legal aspect of it. I want to be with girls I have a good time with and react on the spur of the moment without feeling I have to be with someone. I'm also very independent and I operate on my own quite well. I don't need to have someone with me all the time."

Case in point: his entire staff goes home at night. When Goldstein is in town, he's usually out by the pool, or if the weather doesn't permit, in the den watching TV, basketball most likely.

As it turns out there is someone Goldstein wants to share this all with. When he does pass on, he plans on turning the entire estate over to an institution, "so it can be maintained in the future in this form and be an inspiration, hopefully to people who appreciate good architecture."

Somewhere, John Lautner is smiling in his grave.

BURDENS AND PRIVILEGES

Originally Published in Los Angeles Review of Books

Alan Rifkin has been something of a talismanic figure in my life. I'm sure this is news to him because, despite his generous thanks to me in the back of *Burdens by Water: An Unintended Memoir* for not butchering a couple of his pieces when I was an editor at the *LA Weekly* (it would take a particularly venal editor to manage that trick), we barely know each other. Long before I had the good fortune of working with his prose, though, I had heard of Rifkin by way of an editor who had sponsored both of us many disruptions ago. This editor was known as a writers' editor, and also, perhaps, for having a weakness for "cute-boy" writers, some of whom she praised as "Capital W" writers.

Occasionally, I'd do a piece that got the "Capital W" stamp of approval, but I was generally a benchwarmer on that team. Alan Rifkin was the star. Not long after I'd settled into Los Angeles, my editor friend declared over pancakes that Rifkin was, in fact, her favorite living writer. Considering that some of her other favorite writers at the time included Cormac McCarthy and Martin Amis, that was certainly saying something.

We were at the old Farmers Market on Third and Fairfax long before the days of the Grove, content aggregation and Google analytics. I was relatively new to town and could go to the newsstand there and spend a day thumbing through Los Angeles publications featuring long-form writing that brought the

unfathomable city and its swashbuckling citizens into relief —
treasure maps and pirate tales. Half of the rags were free, and there
was a good chance Rifkin's work was in one of them.

Still, my editor friend's bold declaration made my
pancakes harder to swallow. Is there a more jealous lot than
writers? I poured on the boysenberry and maple syrup and stewed.
Wondering about this Alan Rifkin, I pushed bacon around puddles
of butter and syrup. Obviously, he was a better writer . . . was he
also cuter? Were his gains — as young writers are prone to think
— my losses?

An opportunity to indulge in some welcome
schadenfreude came several years later when the same editor
shepherded into the *LA Weekly* a Fourth of July piece by Rifkin
called "Pool Man." I was then working at *New Times LA*, a
misconceived and misanthropic attempt by a Phoenix-based retail
journalism chain to usurp the shaggy *Los Angeles Reader* and
expand its market share by offering up a cynical cocktail of half-
baked libertarianism and editorial ax-grinding.

At *New Times*, Rifkin's "Pool Man" was held up for
ridicule and trumpeted as an avatar of all that was wrong over there
at the *LA Weakly* [*sic*]. "What is this even about?!" I remember
one of the top editors laughing as he waved the issue around and
predicted that this sort of decadence — 6,000 words about a
fucking pool man! Ha! — spelled the certain end of the *LA Weekly*.
That end, spiritually, if not physically, would come years later
when the same chain took over the *Weekly*, *The Village Voice* and
other fine weeklies and retrofitted them to accommodate its tin-
eared dogma.

Back then, I tried to get with the spirit by summoning
whatever lingering combativeness I could for my old editor
friend's "favorite living writer" and for the paper that published
him. It should have been easy. After all, weren't there important
things going on? The Los Angeles Archdiocese was embroiled in
a grotesque scandal that threatened to take down Cardinal

Mahony; the San Fernando Valley secession movement was gaining steam; and an invasion of Iraq was starting to take on an air of depressing inevitability. Surely 6,000 words on pool men deserved some disdain.

But, I dipped into the story and before long my toes, torso, shoulders and head were fully immersed in a piece published in a local weekly that contained the multitudes of a great novel — looming mortality, social dislocation, individualism versus the yearn for connection, class issues, the question of what amounts to success in our society. Heavy stuff, lightened by Rifkin's supple prose, deep empathy and just the right amount of first-person agency in crafting the narrative:

> *What he liked best about having a pool route was that he was outdoors, and that there were repair problems just tricky enough to challenge him but not defeat him. What I liked best about riding with John was seeing summer arrive one day at a time and watching him listen to the customers talk about their lives —* like Highway to Heaven, *a show I'd never actually seen. Plus it reminded me of the consolation I used to feel working in restaurants on New Year's Eve, to be one of the servers instead of the lonelies at the banquet, with all their good-life expectations.*

It might not have been urgent, but to me it felt essential, and I thought it miraculous that there were places where that level of literary journalism was available for free just about anywhere in the city, including the Farmers Market newsstand. Despite what some of my pseudo-populist *New Times* colleagues may have said about the whole thing, it was the opposite of elitist.

I left for the *LA Weekly* just a couple months after "Pool Man" hit the streets.

***

Among the many functions that Alan Rifkin's *Burdens by Water* serves is to document a time when there was space in our lives and in our media for such ruminative pieces as "Pool Man," or "Swimming with Dolphins" (dolphins as they are), or "Measure the Universe" (the universe as it was), or "The Los Angeles Writing Club" (writers as they hope to be), or "Boys in the Hoods" (monks about to be). The works here mostly span the print boom of the early '90s up through the digital disruptions of more recent vintage. Without belaboring the point, the contemporary structures of publishing have simply made it harder for ace regional writers such as Rifkin to get commissioned far afield to chase stories about ex-pat astronomers in the Atacama Desert or bipeds nosing around with dolphins (and each other) in the Bahamas, or even about born-again Christians in Long Beach who may offer prescriptions for flagging marriages.

These pieces were conceived and birthed when the *LA Weekly*, *Los Angeles Times Magazine*, *L.A. Style*, *California*, *Details* and the like could midwife them. Half of those magazines no longer exist, and the survivors have been made stingy by the digital economy — as have our attention spans. The utilitarian imperative implicit in the whine I heard at that editorial meeting long ago — what's this even about!? — now affects almost every aspect of our lives under the tyranny of almighty Google. The result is that there are fewer opportunities for the kind of writing that Rifkin specializes in. It's a shame, because this blinkered age needs the sort of unifying narratives found in Rifkin's collection more than ever.

But, to proffer a years-late answer to the lingering question: *What's this even about?* I say, *exactly!* Or, *everything!* *Nothing* is fine, too. After all, it's only life, and here in the Western world existential crisis is our birthright whether we like it or not. It may be the one thing we have in common, and ignoring it won't make it go away. (Have you seen the stats on suicide, lately?) The point is, journalism was once allowed and even encouraged to tackle Chekhovian concerns, to give purpose to factual storytelling beyond the mere transfer of information. Rifkin comes from that time, and he did it better than most. This collection is a testament to that.

In lesser hands, of course, these pieces would collapse under their own ambitions, but Rifkin's mastery of narrative architecture and the crystallizing line never let contemplations run away or the prose grow too ponderous. For instance, the "Pool Man" characters mine the "gorgeous crypts" — rectangular, kidney-shaped or "reedy Xanadus" — of their tenuous middle-class lives for signs that their California dream survives.

"To my childhood self," writes Rifkin of actual pool men, "their comings and goings looked like the height of Pied Piper free agency. So much so that decades later, blocked and confused, when the Artist's Way prescribed making list after list of alternative careers, I'd invariably write down: Pool Man."

Burdens by Water's thematic concerns — loss and alienation; the struggle against both — align with canonical Los Angeles literature spanning Fante to Didion and beyond. But unlike many of his fellow "Capital W" Angeleno writers, Rifkin isn't dystopian. As haunted as this collection may be by the specter of Southern California's fading postwar promise — for example, "E Luxo So" is a stunning portrait of the middle-class and the San Fernando Valley losing their respective grips on each other — Rifkin and his subjects are ultimately pursuing moments of grace more than the material signifiers of the good life. "Unless in the guise of a seeker I was really a chameleon, fodder for gangs and cults and whoever loved me most," Rifkin writes in "Consider the Richardsons," his tale of trying to gain surer spiritual footing in deep Christianity.

He often finds what he's looking for in unlikely places: at a basketball game, during which a Dr. J reverse layup transports in "The Metaphysics of Hang Time"; at the Sepulveda Dam, where he attempts firsthand experience of the glory captured by painter Edward Biberman in his collection *Time and Circumstance.*

> *I wanted the dam to have one more chance to perform its optical trick from the freeway, see the periphery glorify the dam, see the era enlarge it — because it isn't possible for anyone but an artist to find the soul of a dam up close, in its gray, cuspid, concrete supports. I mean that I can't say how Biberman did it.*

Rifkin tells me that when he started looking for patterns in his work that might make sense of a collection, he realized these pieces formed a sort of spiritual quest "by a Valley Jew who both grew up and grew old alongside the LA Dream and all its longings for unity." He was relieved, he said, "to see that I'd done a few stories in the past that felt connected in a true, humble way to abiding questions and truths."

It's fitting that the collection resolves with "Writing in the Dust." In the piece, Rifkin puts his auto-ontology to the test, measuring his life as a writer against both history and the encroaching imperatives we spoke of earlier. Does it have and hold meaning, even now? To answer, he must grapple with "the possibly delusional proposition that the conflicts most central to the human condition — truth and illusion, spirit and flesh, heaven and earth, race and community — were reaching an endgame mainly in Los Angeles." In the end, he finds that the burdens of being a Capital W writer in this time and in this place are also its privileges. This collection is proof of that.

FOR THE LOVE OF DESPISED POETRY

Originally published in Los Angeles Review of Books

Scott Timberg took his life on December 10, 2019, a fact that sits with me here unreconciled as I read the posthumously released *Beeswing*, his book with Richard Thompson. I'd probably be thinking of Scott even without this reminder of his passions, as I've thought about him every day since he killed himself, the way you might think of an intimate who suddenly ghosted you. That doesn't make me unique. Scott was widely and deservedly loved, and now he is missed.

I've also thought of him every day since he killed himself in a different way: like the memory of a close call that you can't quite shake. Which is to say, I have some familiarity with the things that troubled Scott and drove him over the edge. This doesn't make me unique either. Scott's downwardly mobile trajectory after reaching the pinnacle of his profession — a fall precipitated by, among other exigencies, the very things he wrote about in his essential *Culture Crash: The Killing of the Creative Class* — is part of a particular zeitgeist. So, no, I'm not unique in the ways the loss of Scott has made me think and feel. But the weariness and grief of this long season increasingly feels to me like it was predicated, if not ushered in, by his death.

The news of his death, like the pandemic that followed, was both shocking and unsurprising. It reached me via a text message that asked a simple question. At the time, I was walking across the campus where I teach, skirting a lush knoll adorned with what I think Scott would agree was better-than-typical public art. A lovely shade tree and the Spanish Revivalist landmark Diehl Hall — a building that, along with Johnny Poet, is Whittier College's most recognizable icon — sat welcomingly atop the hill.

"Weren't you friends with Scott Timberg?" read the text.

In front of me, sunshine reflected optimistically off the glass facade of the shimmering Science & Learning Center, the college's $50 million–plus stake on the future. Behind me, shadows edged across Wardman Library, with its mysterious Nixon Room tucked inside and its great lawn collecting pine needles and students.

The text was an uninvited interloper onto the idyll, and I wasn't thinking at the time of William Carlos Williams' description of "despised poems" — "It is difficult to get the news from poems / yet men die miserably every day / for lack / of what is found there" — though it serves as one of my calls to rally students to the cause of literature, arts and culture.

I wasn't thinking about those lines because in my walking reverie, I'd had a lapse of sorts. I had forgotten what hard times these were for people and poets, had forgotten how little value we placed on those despised poems that Scott loved on a cellular level. But the text jolted me back to reality, and I immediately texted a close friend of ours.

"He didn't kill himself, did he?" I asked.

The question had turned rhetorical before the answer came moments later. For anyone who knew Scott, or had read his work, or had engaged in spirited conversations with him; for anyone who understood how fiercely he defended what is found in those despised poems, and how much the devaluation thereof pained him, the news would not be surprising.

The exhaustion I'd heard in his voice during a recent phone conversation started looping in my head. The familiar, insinuating grin and the conspiratorially cocked eyebrow that I'd encountered at a party some weeks before hijacked my consciousness. That party was the last time I'd seen him alive. It was full of literati. I knew fewer of them than I used to and I spent a good deal of that evening hanging with Scott on the edge of a scene we used to be in the middle of. Scott was reliably generous with his wit, reliably great in conversation — smarter, better versed than anyone — and he, reliably, made me feel relevant.

I put my phone away and continued walking south across campus toward the sunlight that bounced off the Science & Learning Center. The building, a sort of brutalist-modernist mash-up, isn't bad to look at, but the school will be retiring its debt for a long time, maybe even until the humanities, the foundation upon which Whittier College was built, are back en vogue.

No matter. Scott would have loved it here at this little oasis in the middle of Los Angeles County, the home he loved for the existential proposition that it is. Because I'd failed to tell him, though, he never knew that I'd often imagined him here with me or replacing me when I moved on. Aside from everything else — intrepid interlocutor, keen observer, fierce defender of the arts — I have it on good account that Scott was also a great teacher. I think he would have appreciated this place that I believe still understands what happens when our dreams are bereft of poetry.

I also have it on good account (Scott's!) that he was turning into a pretty decent guitar player. If I'm not mistaken, he came to his vision of jukebox herodom late, but in typical fashion, he was earnest in his pursuit, making up for lost time quickly and arriving at proficiency in a blink. He was always working on new chords, new progressions, new songs. In recent years, he'd invited me to jam with him several times, but I had dodged, knowing that despite having decades on him, I wouldn't be able to keep up.

I don't think Scott's growing interest in becoming a musician in his own right was research for *Beeswing*, but I imagine it only enhanced his collaboration with Thompson. It's nice when your heroes are also fellow travelers. Thompson was certainly one of Scott's, and this book rings like the work of people who met on paths that were mysteriously bound for each other, paths that when joined might take them somewhere new and exciting.

Of course, we don't get to see where that new place would be for Scott.

Suicides are personal and unfathomable, and I wouldn't try to explain or characterize Scott's, or anyone else's for that matter. Nor am I trying to make it poetic — it isn't. But I do feel like I know something about how men might suffer for the lack of what is found there in despised poetry — how men trapped in bodies, identities, expectations and projections might feel like there is no way out. Except, perhaps, to somehow become simply spirit. That spirit remains on the pages, in the words he left us, in his stubborn refusal to let us go lacking, in his insistence that we embrace despised poetry and live fully. He's insisting still.

PART FOUR

Creatures Seeking Shelter

"Meanwhile, I wonder if old number
166.614 2554 has found his home."

IKO, IKO!

Originally published in the LA Weekly

My dog, Willa, and I spotted it as we set out on our morning walk.

The thing was ambling slowly, but with an air of determination, across the sidewalk. At first I thought it was something abominable — a giant insect, a tarantula or some other thing that crawls out from under the house and terrorizes the neighborhood (or just me). Willa was circumspect. But like a teenager, I had to have a look.

And what I found upon closer inspection was a fish out of water. Actually, it was a crayfish out of water, otherwise known as a crawfish, or, my favorite name, crawdad. It was dark, about four inches long, with a couple of handsome antennae and menacing pincers out front. Now, crawdads are common to North America, more than half of the 500 species of them reside in our great land, and most of them are found in the Mammoth Caves of Kentucky or in the Mississippi Basin down into Louisiana— which may or may not say something about our muddy national character. But the only place you're likely to see them in my Silver Lake neighborhood is in a painted rendering on the window of Pescado Mojado.

Clearly this crawdad was far from home. How'd it get here? Was it a refugee from Katrina that the local bourgeois liberals at first welcomed with open arms but then cast off, tiring of its *otherness*? I wondered. And wondered even more what to do with it.

There were several options, not the least of which was eating it. I considered selling it to my neighbors, who, if their pack of mutant, little toy dogs is any indication, seem to have an exotic-pet fetish. But the crawdad seemed so helpless and lost that my attention soon turned to matters of its well-being. I went back to my house and got a section of newspaper for it to crawl onto, and then carried it home. I arrived just as my gardener pulled up, so I showed him my morning catch. He held the newspaper and cried "langosta!" to his partner, a little too gleefully. I snatched the crawdad back. It brushed several of its pereiopods (legs) and perhaps even one of its chelipeds (pincers) against me as I held it. I shrieked like a baby and quickly set it down in my front yard. I figured it would like my just-watered grass more than the sidewalk. But then it started its determined hoofing again. Where did it think it was going?

I filled a large, shallow bowl with water and some rocks, but it clambered out as soon as I put it in. I tried flooding a little trough at the edge of the grass and placing it in that. It rested for a minute, but then got up to leave again. Maybe it had errands to run. By this time, I was late for work, so I put it in a muddy bed of greenery in my backyard, figuring it could bury itself if endangered.

All day long, I couldn't stop thinking about my little buddy, wondering what plagues (like my dog or crawfish-eating birds) had set upon it. I found myself growing attached to it. There was something endearing about its purposeful and, let's face it, oblivious manner. At work we thought up names. I liked Iko, from "Iko Iko." *Talkin' 'bout: Hey now! Hey now! / Iko, Iko, unday / Jockamo feeno ai nan / Jockamo fee nan* — the only zydeco song I knew. A co-worker thought of Muddy Waters. I fantasized that I'd come home and find Iko and Willa sipping mint juleps, listening to Dr. John and acting out a scene from *A Streetcar Named Desire*.

It was dark when I got home, and I feared I'd probably seen the last of my crawdad. But I went out back with a flashlight, and there it was in the yard — somehow it had scaled the plant-bed wall and made it down to the grass — just cruising around in his quick-as-molasses fashion. I watered the area and set about eating my Subway six-inch tuna on honey-oat bread with everything on it, plus salt and pepper, oil and vinegar (I recommend). You don't have to be in a hurry when it comes to crawdads, and maybe that's what I liked about Iko.

When I finished eating, I looked out the window and saw Iko hightailing it (literally, his tail was up) for a ditch Willa had dug that leads under the side wall and out into the front yard. Once again, it had set a course for the dangerous world beyond my sanctuary. Still, I figured I had 10 minutes before this was an emergency.

So I called up my friend John and asked him to join me in a mission to release Iko into Echo Park Lake. John said he and his wife would be proud to join in such a noble cause. For maximum stealth, we dressed in dark clothes and wore hats. I retrieved Iko from my driveway and put him in a large bucket of water and mud, which I hoped would ease the trauma motor transport might cause the little guy.

We parked on the north end of the lake and, with the bucket held closely to my chest, made it about 10 yards before a film-crew security guy started hollering at us. Apparently the place was on lockdown for the next day's shoot. Time was of the essence. Radios started cackling. Helicopters buzzed overhead. We could no longer steal through the park; we had to scurry. We lost precious moments bickering about the best place to set Iko free — there were things like currents, ducks and turtles to consider, and no lily pads in sight. Finally, we found a reasonably sheltered pool on the northwest end and let Iko go. He quickly disappeared into the murk.

Unsure of Iko's fate, we drove home in somber silence. I think. I can't be sure. My hat had furry earflaps and I couldn't hear!much!anyway.

THE TORTOISE AND THE TANK

Originally published in the LA Weekly

Sand in the Box

The worst sandstorm in John Wagstaffe's memory is at full howl. We're deep inside Iraq, somewhere between the towns of Medina Jabal and Medina Wasl, on a day when the threat of violence is as thick as the squalls of sand. But there's something about the way Wagstaffe never goes anywhere without a carton of cigarettes that inspires, if not confidence, then something like good cheer. Even as the sandstorm reaches a blinding rage, Wagstaffe, our military handler, maintains the upbeat demeanor of a tour guide. Until, that is, we lose sight of the vehicle in front of us and drive off the shallow and slightly smoothed path in the desert sand that serves as our road.

Our caravan is three-strong. The lead vehicle, like ours, is a white van with a U.N. sign in the front and back windows. The signs are meant to indicate we're not fair game, though, as Wagstaffe warns, indiscriminate IEDs don't pay attention to such warnings. Following us is a blue SUV carrying a documentary team from Sweden. They have no signs.

We find our way back to the road, but the sandstorm raises a couple of issues. Veering off the path again could send us into a ditch or, perhaps, into one of the phantom Humvees that patrol the fringes of this sand-clouded route like sharks in murky water. Or maybe we'll just hit the van in front of us, or be hit by the SUV from the rear. Wagstaffe isn't exactly flustered, but he is a bit less unflappable than usual. I suggest that he radio the van in front of us to tell the driver to put on its hazard lights so we have something to follow.

"That would be great," he tells me, "but we don't have any radios."

Sweet, I think, the world's last dollar is going to be spent out here, but we don't have walkie-talkies.

When we careen off the road again, the caravan stops and we wait until the sandstorm lets up enough for us to find the road back to Medina Wasl. I'm worried we're going to miss the firefight that's rumored to be taking place in less than a half-hour.

We crossed over the Kuwaiti border and into Iraq earlier this morning, June 4, 2008, at 10:40 a.m. There's a military designation for that time but damned if I know what it is. After a quick debriefing from Wagstaffe and a successful negotiation of a checkpoint on the outskirts of the main base, we're bound for the heart of what's known as The Box — 1,200 square miles of sand, hills and shrub as far as the eye can see, occasionally interrupted by a mountain range or a spectral Hummer with a .50-caliber machine gun on top. The Box is where the shit goes down, and, if all goes as planned, we'll be there to see it.

A mile or two into Iraq, proceeding east, Wagstaffe points out a mosque on a hill. "It's where the Muslims go to pray," he says. "It also gets blown up periodically."

Not long after, we approach Medina Wasl, a village that comprises 70 percent Sunnis and 30 percent Shiites. Medina Wasl is little more than a stretch of primitive buildings along a main street. Like so many towns and villages in Iraq, it has its problems.

"Massive unemployment, insurgent activity, sectarian violence," says Wagstaffe, before adding cheerily, "normally, on Wednesday night they slice the imam's throat."

Wagstaffe is a crusty denizen of this here desert and a salty vet of this man's army. He was Colin Powell's spokesman back when the good general ran the show, and can't say enough positive things about our former secretary of state. Especially when it comes to Powell's facility with the internal-combustion mechanics of his favorite automobile, the Volvo. According to Wagstaffe, the general was practically a certified Volvo mechanic. Ah, if only he could read intelligence reports as well as car manuals . . . but that's another story.

As far as this one goes, I want to say up front that Wagstaffe is a good egg and whatever happens out here in the desert is not his fault. He's a good egg and a ripe red tomato. At least, his sun-blasted skin is the color of a ripe red tomato, an impression made all the more vivid by the shock of blond hair on top of his tomato face.

We park outside the village walls and proceed on foot. A couple of U.S. soldiers huddled on each side of a short alley between buildings politely but firmly ask us to get the hell out of the way. We slither past the soldiers and move down the main street, keeping close to the buildings. The tension is thick; the street is strangely still. Soldiers point rifles down the middle of the road and watch for anything suspicious-looking. Wagstaffe is less demure than his guests and strolls out into the fray like he's bulletproof. He waves me over to talk with one of the less-harried-looking soldiers, S.Sgt. Lewis Maffei, an Observer Controller — a higher-ranking combat vet here assessing U.S. troops' performance.

"There was a guy wearing a vest with explosives. He got through security, where [the commander of the U.S. troops] was having a briefing with the mayor, and blew himself up," says Maffei, who's done three tours in Iraq, has seen this sort of thing before and is very businesslike about it all. He gives me a casualty report: one U.S. soldier wounded, two Iraqi army killed, one Iraqi civilian killed and four wounded.

The town is on lockdown and the soldiers on the ground — members of the 2nd Heavy Brigade Combat Team, 1st Infantry

Division, out of Fort Riley, Kansas — are engaged in critical responses that require coordination, precision and clear thinking. The town has to be secured, the citizens calmed. There is an Iraqi doctor in town, but following local customs a female doctor — in this case a U.S. servicewoman — must be brought in to attend to the women. Casualties are being flown out. It's all happening at once. It's intense, but the trick is to keep it from getting any tenser.

"This town was neutral when [the U.S. troops] first showed up," Maffei tells me. "They have water problems, power problems, things like that. If the unit helps them, then they go to the positive side. If they treat them badly, or lie to them, they go to the negative side, and the bad guys start recruiting more people."

These soldiers have been in the country for a month now, and engaged in full-spectrum operations for two weeks. They're relatively raw and untested, but days like this one will teach them fast. Capt. Andy Kaiser, another Observer Controller on hand who has two tours under his belt, tells me that scenarios like this one immediately raise the most fundamental question — whether to stay or go.

"I always stood my ground, versus leaving," Kaiser says. "Because the whole insurgent thing is to get us to move and show that we're scared . . . [The commanding officer] has decided he's going to stay today and keep security and keep treating people. That's the right decision. You don't want to run from these guys. We've got up-armored vehicles, tanks, fighting vehicles — you leave, you know, it gives a bad impression."

When the immediate threat dies down, I'm taken to meet Bassan Kalasho, the provincial governor of Ghazi. He is monitoring the action and acting as the surrogate for the 275 Iraqis in this town. He's the guy sitting on the tinderbox. I ask him how it's going so far.

"The brigade commander is doing a great job and the soldiers are doing an excellent job," says Kalasho with the calm demeanor of someone who's been to this rodeo a few times before. "Two days ago, they caught 27 from al Qaeda and 17 from Mahdi [Shiite cleric Muqtada al-Sadr's paramilitary force]. They have an engineer company here. They already rebuilt the middle of Medina Wasl. Security is the main issue here. If we don't get security, we can't rebuild Iraq."

As the calamity, similar to so many others across Iraq since this war began, settles into the steady, methodical pace of a crime-scene investigation, we drive on to Medina Jabal. A canteen there serves up some good American-style eats. But on the way out of Medina Wasl, we run over something that causes our van to slightly lurch.

"Was that an IED?" asks the director of the Swedish documentary team, who is riding in our van.

"Could be," says Wagstaffe, who presses on. "Or it could be someone fucking with us with an RPG."

"I think it was a cardboard box," I say.

Nobody in the van subscribes to this theory. They want to be part of the drama.

***

We move on across the desert to Medina Jabal. When we pull into town, a collection of drab stone buildings that could serve as the set for a Western, Wagstaffe points out the jail. We park near the cemetery and unload. The wind is picking up. The air is thick with sand. The first thing we come upon is a blown-down palm tree, about 40 feet long and four feet around.

"We were guaranteed these palm trees wouldn't blow over," Wagstaffe says.

Most of the townspeople are covered from head to toe in traditional robes, their mouths and noses protected from the sand. They are moving inside for cover. We duck into the cantina, which evokes that famous bar scene from *Star Wars*. Villagers, insurgents, soldiers, all are taking a break from the day to order tacos, burgers and hot dogs. At 12:30 p.m. — and damned if I know the military designation for that time — the local mosque's bells chime.

"They have to play that music five times a day," Wagstaffe says.

Nobody is bowing toward Mecca.

We order our food and take a seat at a table with Puff, an insurgent. Puff has been out here for three years. He is eating tacos. Puff has beautiful blue eyes, dark hair — well, mostly dark, some swaths are grayish — and his skin is a mix of peach pigmentation interrupted by large, growing patches of darker pigment, like birthmarks. He says he's turning black and that his doctors don't know why.

"I'm the first person on record with this," Puff tells me. "They estimate that by the time I'm 60, I'll be a full-fledged black man."

He says that with his condition and all, this is the only place that would accept him as he is, no questions asked. Last night, as he slept, Special Forces raided his hut. They shot him three times in the chest. Then they asked if he agreed that he was dead.

"Yes," he said, "I agree that I'm dead."

Then, for extra measure, they shot him a few times in the balls.

"Special Forces can be dicks," he says.

Puff is married. He says he spent $49,000 on his fiancée's engagement ring. He isn't leaving this circus anytime soon. In fact, he says, he has orders to go to Fort Bragg to get Airborne training. After that, he'll be in the shit for real. He's not stoked.

We hit the road, heading back to Medina Wasl. The sand is blowing so thick, we can barely make out the village until we're right upon it, and then it appears mostly as a silhouette. Everyone's taken cover except for a team of U.S. troops on the south side of town.

Wagstaffe opts to sit this one out, but photographer C.R. Stecyk III and I hop out of the van and move toward a group of U.S. forces hovering around a wounded insurgent. Apparently, we missed the firefight, but not by much. Other troops are taking up strategic positions that offer cover and a clear shot at anything moving on the perimeter. Humvees, tanks, armored personnel carriers scramble for position. A tank pulls up feet from us, along with a Humvee full of soldiers. The guy handling the .50-caliber machine gun shouts out, "If anything moves, I'll paste the fucking city." I believe him.

After a tense hour or so, the insurgents are caught, and the town is cleared. The men of the 2nd Heavy Brigade Combat Team, 1st Infantry Division, out of Fort Riley — the Big Red One — retire to the Forward Operating Base for some rest and shelter.

"Cool kicks," one of them shouts out to me as I walk past, obviously pleased with my red Converse One-Stars.

By now, you may have guessed that we aren't really in Iraq but a reasonable facsimile, where the palm trees are reinforced with two-by-fours and the bad guys, like Puff the pretend insurgent, belong to the 2,500-strong 11th Armored Cavalry Regiment. Here at Fort Irwin, California, home of the Army's National Training Center, America's soldiers play out their most realistic live-fire exercises on a piece of the Western Mojave Desert as big as Rhode Island and getting bigger as the mission expands.

The Long March Home

In another part of this desert, on a different day, a male, 60 or so years old by the looks of him (official designation: 166.614 2554), is on the run. Like so many refugees in this world, he's just trying to find home. But it's going to be hard. For one thing, he's in the middle of desolate and unfamiliar terrain. It's a hot day and he probably doesn't quite have his bearings just yet — understandable, considering he's been dropped off here in the middle of nowhere by helicopter. His quest for home would take him over miles of unforgiving land, rugged mountains, and expose him to harsh elements and unsympathetic predators or vehicles that could crush him without even seeing him. Not to mention he's just not cut out for this kind of thing. He's a slow and steady sort, and, watching him plod across a dry wash, one foot in front of the other, it's hard not to be a bit moved by his determination.

All the more heartrending is the fact that, try as he might, the truth is he isn't ever going home again. The place he came from, where he lived his entire life, is fenced off. Even if his heart were really set on it, he'd make just a little more than a kilometer a day. And he probably wouldn't want to stay if he did make it, because things aren't ever going to be the same back home. His land is needed — for dubious or essential purposes, depending on your politics — by newcomers further up the food chain. I wouldn't bet against him surviving, though. His type has been around for a million years. He's a beautiful, distinguished-looking fellow . . . all 15 inches of him. Did I mention he's a tortoise?

One of nearly 700 California desert tortoises, a species listed as threatened under the federal and state Endangered Species Act, number 166.614 2554 is being flown off the reservation, so to speak. Along with 40 other tortoises today, he's been dropped off in this sector of the Mojave, about 20 miles east and 10 miles north of Barstow, for relocation — away from the home he's known all of his life: Fort Irwin, California. It's all part of the first and largest military-sponsored tortoise airlift in history. Which makes him collateral damage in a war far different from the one the soldiers were preparing for in Medina Wasl.

For years, the tanks of Fort Irwin and the California desert tortoise of the Western Mojave have lived together in relative peace. Recently, however, the détente has blown up, and, like many conflicts around the world, it's territorial.

See, the National Training Center at Fort Irwin needs more land. One reason is that brigade-sized training exercises involve significant man- and machine power, usually 4,000 to 5,000 soldiers, plus all their equipment — tanks, artillery, transport vehicles, armored vehicles, etc. Another significant factor is that the distance in which our armed forces can engage the enemy has increased from ranges of up to 12 miles in 1980, when the center was designated, to up to 60 miles now. Also, tactical operations move at a much quicker pace than they used to, from about a 10 mph average to 25 mph these days. Thus the 100 Hours War, as the Persian Gulf invasion is sometimes called. Indeed, the effectiveness of Gulf War I is often credited to the training our troops did at Fort Irwin.

Unfortunately for number 166.614 2554, the land the military covets is one of the few areas where the California desert tortoise has thrived in recent decades. Now, the land has become a political and environmental battlefield. On one side is the welfare of our soldiers; on the other, according to its defenders, is the future of one of the planet's oldest species.

Fort Irwin, in one form or another, has been lurking just beyond the Los Angeles Basin, not far past the Cajon Pass, somewhat out of sight and somewhat out of mind for nearly 70 years. In 1940, President Roosevelt established a military reservation of some 1,000 square miles, where Fort Irwin now exists, in a vast expanse of the Mojave Desert. It was originally called the Mojave Anti-Aircraft Range and was renamed Camp Irwin in honor of Maj. Gen. G. Leroy Irwin, the World War I commander of the 57th Field Artillery Brigade in 1942. Contrary to lore, Gen. Patton did not train there. The camp was deactivated in 1944 and then reactivated in 1951 to train combat units for the Korean War.

The base was designated Fort Irwin in 1961. Artillery and engineer units were deployed directly to Vietnam from Fort Irwin during that war. In the '70s, the post was semi-retired and used by National Guard and Army Reserve units. In 1980, its fortunes reversed when it was selected to become the site of the new National Training Center.

"All the American units that went to the Gulf War went through here," Wagstaffe tells me. "We had the best Republican Guard in the world." And in the '80s, when the final showdown was going to be with the Soviet Union, Wagstaffe says, "we had the best Soviet unit in the world — including any in the Soviet Union." (Of course, given the fresh conflict between Russia and Georgia, one could argue that the Army needs to get busy bringing back some of those old Soviet units.)

Fort Irwin is the only training area in the world that can handle force-on-force, live-fire war games for heavy brigade-sized military forces. Training generally takes place over a 28-day rotation, the final two weeks of which are realistic war games that try to prepare soldiers for the types of scenarios they will encounter in places like Afghanistan and Iraq. Wagstaffe says that the unit out of Fort Riley, nearing the end of its training cycle during our visit, will soon be deployed to Iraq — as early as September or December.

The base is under the command of an up-and-comer named Brig. Gen. Dana Pittard, a West Point grad who, like the soldiers now in training, started his career with Fort Riley's 1st Infantry Division. A vet of both Operation Desert Storm and Operation Iraqi Freedom, Pittard was a military aide to President Clinton and is a tank-warfare expert, which makes him well suited for his current post.

Entering Fort Irwin is a surreal experience. There's a whole world out there far from the average citizen's view. The base itself is the size of a small city — hosting 20,000 people during the day, 9,000 at night. Attention to detail is astounding —

the mosques, the urban areas made to simulate Iraqi villages, the role players inhabiting those villages, the fake palm trees that sometimes blow over in sandstorms. When they first started making over The Box to provide the mix of urban and desert warfare we now find ourselves engaged in, Wagstaffe tells me, the Army bought every shed available from Shed World, with major operations in nearby Hesperia, Victorville and Apple Valley, to start building the towns.

"It cost a lot of money," says Wagstaffe.

Even so, Brig. Gen. Pittard wasn't satisfied with the look and feel (Wagstaffe remembers him saying, "You think this looks like Iraq?"), and set up a competition among three Hollywood movie-set operations. The winner got to turn The Box into Iraq. Currently, Fort Irwin is constructing a $57 million replica of Fallujah, which we drive by in its nascent state on our way back from that lunch in Medina Jabal.

"It's going to be the largest urban-warfare facility in the world," says Wagstaffe, proudly. "We import the stones from Iraq."

"Why?" I ask.

"I don't know," he says.

It doesn't stop there. Occupying the Iraqi villages are 250 Iraqi "actors" like Bassan Kalasho, the provincial governor. These actors stay 24/7 during the full training rotation, often under harsh conditions: heat, sandstorms, bitter nights and boredom. They man their posts — as governors, mayors, villagers, merchants, doctors, shepherds, imams – all day long, whether they are due to see any action that day or not.

"They do it out of a sense of patriotism," says Wagstaffe, "for their former country and their adopted country."

Kalasho is indicative of these people. During Saddam's reign, the Baath Party killed Kalasho's parents. "I do everything here, not just play governor. I teach a culture class," he says. "If we can save one innocent life, on both sides, that will be great for us."

The Army has also hired 300 unemployed people from Barstow ("the Barstow 300," Wagstaffe calls them), at $4,000 a month, to fill out the role-playing. While it's certainly a small boon to the local economy, Wagstaffe admits it's barely made a dent in the area's unemployment rate.

The idea is to be as realistic as possible in every phase of warfare. When soldiers die in simulated combat, they are taken away to someplace called Deadland. Commanding officers must then go through the process of condolences, requesting awards, requisitions.

IEDs are made with Iraqi phones and simulators. Real amputees are brought in from Hollywood to play casualties. Fake shepherds bring their goats and sheep to market. Prisoners go to court and are represented by lawyers. Imams get their throats sliced. Poker games between Sunni and Shia strongmen go awry. Vendettas are played out. One gets the impression that this is the largest movie set in the world.

The operating budget for Fort Irwin must be staggering. I ask Wagstaffe what it is.

"I don't know," he says. "A lot."

I'm not the only one waiting for the numbers. Wagstaffe tells me later that Dan Rather is still waiting on the info. "If I ever find it," he says, "I'll get it to you guys." Me first, I assume.

What does it mean when our financial system is collapsing, when there's no money for basic infrastructure, social services, health care and education, but there's a never-ending pipeline of green to the military? I have no fucking idea, but maybe the desert tortoise — pushed to the brink of collapse itself, and now being airlifted out of a critical habitat so a military base can play more and bigger war games — would tell us if it could talk. Since it can't, we go searching for answers in Barstow, of all places.

Road Warriors

My sun-absorbing black Jeep Cherokee is in four-wheel drive and moving at a righteous clip through the Mojave. It's all good sport in a delirious *Mad Max* kind of way, until my partner in crime, C.R. Stecyk III, and I realize we have no idea where we are. We also have no detailed map, no shovel to dig ourselves out should we get bogged down in the sand, a temporary spare that wouldn't be much good out here, barely half a tank of gas and precious little water. What brought us here is the kind of impulse that can get you into trouble in the desert.

This whole adventure started back in early April, when I finally succumbed to Stecyk, an intrepid artist, photographer and cultural historian who looks at the universe and sees patterns and connections that weave themselves into an inevitable design while the rest of us, caught up in the fabric, see only randomness and coincidence. These patterns and designs he sees sometimes take on a sinister, *X-Files*-like shape and tone colored in a military-industrial palette.

Not surprisingly, Stecyk spends a lot of time in the desert. Often, when he reports back after such trips, eager to describe the tangled web, I'll put the phone down and pick it up at what I believe are the appropriate intervals to insert an "umm hmmm . . ." or ". . . really?"

During one of these phone calls, when he was going on about a huge tortoise relocation being done by the military and what this action said about where we are at this time in our history — or something like that — I suggested we go out to take a look. It wasn't that I was so interested in desert tortoises — I wasn't even aware that they were endangered, or that they were our official state reptile, or that they could somehow be part of the Rorschach test some people, like Stecyk, see when they visit the desert just beyond the tentacles of our metropolis. I just didn't have anything better to do.

The day of my first descent into this parallel universe begins very early after a near-sleepless night. I pick up Stecyk in West Los Angeles by 6:30 a.m. There's a military designation for that time, but I don't think I'm ever going to learn this math. As Stecyk packs his gear into my Cherokee, I notice he looks a bit like a tortoise himself — long neck, hairless head, thick skin. I try not to make too much of it as we head east on I-10. In the weeks that follow, I try not to make much of the fact that nearly everyone I meet in the tortoise-saving business begins to look like one.

Our plan is . . . well, we don't have much of a plan except to try to crash whatever party might be going on out in the desert. But we do have a destination: Barstow. As anyone who has traveled from there to Las Vegas knows, Barstow is a portal into all kinds of weirdness. Out there are military bases, ghost towns, mines, meth labs, bikers and escape artists of all sorts. And somewhere in the desert surrounding that town, Stecyk has heard, tortoises are being bagged and tagged for relocation off a huge military base I know nothing about.

On the way, Stecyk tells a story about taking his kid out to the desert near Edwards Air Force Base (mascot, Eddie the Desert Tortoise) in 1997 to see Chuck Yeager break the sound barrier on the 50th anniversary of the first time he made history. (The general did the same thing in 2007 to commemorate the 60th anniversary.)

As we drive farther, Stecyk, whose son is now a lieutenant stationed in Iraq, fills my head with ideas about how we're surrounded by military bases bent on expansion. But he didn't always think this. When the Cold War was first over and won, he thought, like a lot of us did, that we were at the beginning of a remarkable and unprecedented event in which an empire, ours, would voluntarily draw down its military at the height of its power and invest in peace instead of war. We called it the peace dividend, and the potential implications for our country and the world were as vast as they were benign. In 2000, our budget surplus was a record $230 million. It was expected to go up by another trillion over the next 10 years. We had just made the largest payment of our national debt in history.

Our priorities, it seemed, were shifting. A new era of investment in education, infrastructure, civil society — the world — was at hand. Then came September 11 and everything after. Our deficit is now approaching $500 billion and our national long-term debt has nearly doubled to more than $9 trillion (adding more than a billion a day) since Bill Clinton left office. We're fighting incredibly expensive wars in ways that seem to ensure no end. And, we're completely out of money.

"We're so fucking fucked, it's almost meaningless," laughs Stecyk. "But not the military. It's bombs away with them."

Where it once looked like the great bases would be mothballed or put to other uses, now they are expanding and consuming and surrounding us. Or so it seems when you start looking for patterns.

When you step back and think about it from the long view, or just get out a map instead, what Stecyk says begins to make sense. Just a little north of Lancaster is the 301,000-acre Edwards Air Force Base, the most fabled flight-test center in the world. Continue north on the 395 to Ridgecrest and you run into China Lake Naval Air Weapons Testing Center, a behemoth weapons-development and -testing range taking up some million acres (1,723 square miles) of the Mojave Desert 75 miles north of Barstow. Fort Irwin's National Training Center abuts China Lake on its eastern border. Head south a bit from there and you have the Marine Corps Logistics Base on the south side of Barstow. Go east about 35 miles on I-40 and you run into the Marine Corps Air Ground Combat Center in Twentynine Palms. These bases form a nearly contiguous desert perimeter around greater metropolitan Los Angeles — indeed, military operations account for one-third of the Mojave's land — making this one of the most highly militarized zones in the world. Throw in Point Mugu Naval Air Station in Ventura and Camp Pendleton Marine Corps Base in

North County, San Diego, and we're surrounded on all sides by military operations. This is an oft-overlooked aspect of our existence here. Some of these bases want to get bigger — foremost among them, Fort Irwin, within whose southern boundary that old chap number 166.614 2554 used to reside.

Stecyk and I make it to the Starbucks near the Tanger Outlet Center in Barstow by about 9 a.m. That's 0900 to you civvies (I guess I'm learning this new math after all). I pay for a Wi-Fi card to look online for anything that will point us in the direction of the soon-to-be-displaced tortoises. But first, I ask the barista if she knows where the tortoises are.

"They're in the outlet stores," she says.

This seems like her final answer, so we go to the Internet.

We find the address of the nearby district headquarters of the Bureau of Land Management and decide to drop in. The building is standard-issue Western-state modern bureaucracy — A-frame, earth tones and glass. A big flag flaps in the wind out front. The parking lot is empty. The streets are empty. Everything is still except for the wind, which whistles hot and empty through our ears. It's as if a neutron bomb has gone off in this town.

Oh, yeah, it's Sunday. The BLM office is closed.

We set out for a pet store in a mini-mall just down the way. Surely some granola-eating pet-store person with a heart of gold will know what's up with these tortoises. But the pet store is also closed.

So we head down I-10 toward Needles, where there's an animal-rescue center. Surely *here* some granola-eating animal-rescue person with a heart of gold will be suffering the tortoises. And, in fact, the rescue center, in a bleak strip next to a gravel quarry, is staffed by an attractive young woman who fits the bill . . . but she doesn't know shit about tortoises, and rightly thinks we're fools. When we ask for directions to the Desert Discovery Center, which supposedly has some tortoises in a man-made habitat, the woman looks like she wants to kill us with contempt.

Then a tatted-up young gangbanger in a black bandanna hauls in a couple of frothing pit bulls . . . it's time for us to be going anyway.

Back out on 40 East, in search of the Desert Discovery Center, we see the Marine Corps Logistics Base. Surely there are no granola eaters with hearts of gold, but we decide to take our chances. At the gate, a guard who is all business asks what ours is. We tell him we're looking for the tortoises being relocated — does he know anything about it? Weirdly, recognition flashes in his eyes, and he tells us to wait right there. He comes back with a local newspaper article about the project. Apparently, we missed media day by about 24 hours. The Marine pulls out a map, points us in the general vicinity of Fort Irwin Road, which will take us back to the highway home, and wishes us good luck. We pull off a few yards down the road to read the article but are interrupted by a firm knock on the window. The guard wants us off his base.

We drive north on Fort Irwin Road, sure that somewhere out there are tortoises in peril. We're pretty sure we can't save them, but we wouldn't mind seeing one. After several miles, we pass the Calico Mountains and hang a hard right down what might very well be private access to a rancher's homestead. We blow by that, and before we know it, we're somewhere out on Coyote Lake, a large, dry lakebed between Barstow and Baker, in the vicinity of the southern reaches of Fort Irwin. We follow what seems to be a path across the lakebed. I feel full of purpose, capable of anything. I am the *Road Warrior*. ("Two days ago, I saw a rig that can 'aul that tanker . . . you wanna get out of 'ere, you talk to me . . .") But my reverie is soon interrupted by worry about where this thing is going and how the hell we'll get out of there should something go awry. We don't have enough water to hike out and the sun is singing "Mad Dogs and Englishmen." I've become the Road Worrier.

Suddenly, the path spits us out onto a larger, wider route that's obviously used for heavy machinery. We stop at this strange crossroads marked only by lava rock, sand, distant vistas and a change in the ground from soft to hard. I climb on top of the Jeep for a look. Nothing but desert as far as the eye can see. Stecyk tries to get the GPS in his cell phone to work. No dice. We sit there for a minute and debate going back the way we came, defeated, or continuing on this new road to nowhere. Then, just a cloud of dust at first, I notice a pickup truck coming toward us.

I jump off the Jeep and wave down the truck. A young man and woman are in the cab, and there's a bunch of gear in the bed covered with a camper top. I ask if they've been camping.

"No," says the guy. "We're biologists working on this desert tortoise project . . ."

What are the chances?

We identify ourselves as journalists up from Los Angeles, trying to get a handle on this whole tortoise-relocation thing, and that's when our new best friends get a little cagey. Apparently, we shouldn't be here and they shouldn't be answering media questions. But bless their hearts, they don't want to leave us to our fates out here in the desert — they point us in the general direction of the field headquarters for the folks rounding up tortoises in this area. The directions are a little dicey — of the up-over-yonder sort — so we give them a head start and start tailing them. A few miles of up and over and yonder ensue, and then they lose us.

Somehow, we find the field headquarters. But there are no biologists in sight. There's a trailer, with the door flapping in the wind, some portable restroom facilities and just a few other signs of life. But right when we think our luck is up, we notice a green Subaru approaching. Inside is a comely young biologist, who apparently didn't get the memo about how we're not supposed to be here. She gladly escorts us to a processing center out in the field, where tortoises are being readied for relocation.

A few fieldworkers are huddled under a tarp when we arrive. They are weighing, measuring and putting a transmitter on a good-sized male, probably middle-aged. The tortoise will then be put in a plastic crate with water until he's relocated. They tell us over the past two years they've counted nearly 800 tortoises that need to be moved. We ask what they think about this whole thing — moving hundreds of tortoises like this. They're reluctant to talk, but the gist of what they do say is that the tortoises had a good deal here because they've been living on military land that restricted public use. Their new home will not have nearly as many restrictions, they say, and we get the general feeling they don't think it's such a good deal for the tortoises.

"I don't think that [the new] habitat is as good," says a guy who tells us he's been hired for the project mostly because he's a desert rat who knows the terrain well. "There are power lines and all-terrain vehicles and a lot more desert use there — off-roaders, hikers, campers."

Why, we ask, is this being done?

"I think a lot of it is just the times," he says.

Before we can get into it much further, an official-looking vehicle appears in the distance, winding its way through the mountain roads.

"Do you think they're here for us?" I ask Stecyk.

"Of course they are," he says. "They can read your license plate from outer space. They probably know who you are, where you live and what you're about. I'm surprised it's taken this long for them to get here."

A couple of stern-looking officials pull up and ask us to leave. They point us toward a more user-friendly road out of the wilderness that will lead us to I-15 and back to Barstow. On the way, we pass signs informing us that vehicles shouldn't enter this area without official military escort, and others that say *Tank Crossing*.

We take the old Route 66 back to Barstow. Amid the kitsch and blight, we come upon a carport motel laid out like a wheel that seems to be a live-in art project where vintage cars reside, and maybe even some people too. The entire structure, though, is designed to showcase and accommodate the cars. Human habitation is definitely secondary. We duck into the Googie-era Denny's next door, clean and burnished, pristine in attention to period detail. I'm looking out the window, rapt with the incongruity of it all, feeling lighted by this otherworld, when I notice a tweaked-out pregnant woman stumbling her way up the street, trailed by a guy drinking something out of a brown bag.

After lunch, we finally find the Desert Discovery Center, famous to some degree as the home of a 38-by-30-inch chunk of rock known as the Old Woman Meteorite. It's the second-largest meteorite in the U.S. and weighs three tons. The Discovery Center is also home of the Mojave Desert Puppet Theater. We miss that show, but the tortoise habitat is out back and it's feeding time. An attractive woman (I'm beginning to wonder what's in the water out here) puts out a lunch of cabbage and other greens for the two males that live there in a state of uneasy détente.

"They fight a lot," she tells me, and it seems clear she cares.

I ask her what got her interested in the plight of the desert tortoises.

"Probation," she tells me. "I have to volunteer here for my community service."

Alternative Rock and a Hard Place

"So," says John Wagstaffe by way of greeting, "you are the guys who were driving around lost in the desert a couple weeks ago."

Wagstaffe can't help himself. Seems word of our desert misadventure has trickled up the ranks. It's several weeks after our initial tortoise quest and a couple of weeks before he will take us into The Box when Stecyk and I first meet our sun-dried tour guide at a Holiday Inn on the western end of Barstow. Good egg that he is, though, Wagstaffe seems eager to get us out for an official visit with the tortoises. The translocation of nearly 600 tortoises from a

36-square-mile tract at the very southern tip of Fort Irwin, known as the Southern Expansion Area, is in its final stages. The tortoises are being placed on 13 different square-mile plots. Land use here is restricted to some degree, but it's not completely off-limits.

This Southern Expansion translocation is the first of three being planned, and it's already a year behind the Army's schedule. The next phases are the western expansion, which includes the controversial Superior Valley tract, where the largest population of tortoises lives, and the Eastgate parcel, on the fort's eastern frontier. Study of this initial translocation is considered imperative to the success of future efforts, though everyone acknowledges that those will take place before the long-term effects of this first move are fully understood.

The expansion drive started back in the mid-'80s, when the Army decided that changes in war doctrine, tactics and equipment meant that the National Training Center at Fort Irwin needed about 193,000 more acres. This happened to coincide with a downturn in the fortunes of the California desert tortoises, especially the Western Mojave population. For nearly two decades, the main obstacle to Fort Irwin's growth has been the desert tortoise.

Ironically, desert tortoises look like little tanks, with hard shells and a protruding appendage out front — the gular horn. They've been in this desert for a long, long time. And they're very territorial and homebound. The reptiles spend 95 percent of their time underground and come up to eat, mate and occasionally fight. They find a place that works for them, dig a burrow with their clawed front feet, and stick with it. They build catch basins for infrequent rainwater and can be found waiting at them before it rains. Their bladders can store, conserve and distribute water throughout their bodies for up to a year.

But even with these survival characteristics, their existence is in jeopardy. In some areas of the Mojave, where populations have been studied closely, they've declined by up to 90 percent. A major culprit in these study areas has been a contagious upper-respiratory disease. All sorts of factors, though, have contributed to the tortoises' general fall: livestock grazing, which depletes the food supply; development, which attracts ravens that prey on tortoise eggs; off-road vehicles, which damage burrows or even crush the tortoises; and predation from coyotes, Gila monsters, foxes and other animals.

The decline in desert-tortoise populations, especially in the Western Mojave — near total in some areas where the tortoise had been common as recently as the 1970s — led to the species being listed as endangered in 1989. That status was changed to "threatened" the following year. This listing happened to coincide with the Gulf War (the one managed by Wagstaffe's favorite Volvo mechanic), and threw a roadblock in front of Fort Irwin's increasingly urgent expansion hopes. The land on the fringes of Fort Irwin is one of the few places where the tortoise population has done well, largely because the area is remote and closed off to many of the aforementioned threats.

When the expansion idea started to gather steam, negotiations began between the Army and the Bureau of Land Management — which has jurisdiction over much of the Mojave lands, and is charged with making sure Fort Irwin's development complies with tortoise-conservation efforts under the Endangered Species Act.

In 1991, the Army came up with what was called the Modified Coyote Basin Alternative, a proposed 328,660-acre annexation primarily to the south, southwest and southeast of the fort's boundaries. This plan was stymied when the U.S. Fish and Wildlife Service, the ultimate arbiter of species management, said in a draft biological opinion on the plan (one that was never finalized) that the expansion would threaten the tortoises' existence.

The Army came back with a new proposal, called the Silurian Valley Alternative, which would have directed expansion further to Fort Irwin's north, east and southern boundaries, in desert lands closer to Baker than Barstow. Fish and Wildlife got on board for this plan, in part because it was well-removed from Superior Valley, which on a map looks like the final piece of a puzzle that would connect Fort Irwin along its southwest border with China Lake Naval Weapons Center. Superior Valley is one of the rare places in the Western Mojave where tortoises thrive, and this plan would leave it unmolested. But the Army subsequently decided the terrain wasn't suitable, some say because of well-trafficked roads in and out of Baker.

Meanwhile, plans mandated by the Endangered Species Act and other environmental laws to protect the tortoises were being drawn up. In 1994, the U.S. Fish and Wildlife Service issued the *Desert Tortoise (Mojave Population) Recovery Plan*, which recommended six critical habitat areas, known as recovery units. The Western Mojave Recovery Unit is one of them. Within that recovery unit, several Desert Wildlife Management Areas (DWMAs) were proposed, among them a vast swath of desert labeled the Superior-Cronese Desert Management Area and the Superior-Cronese Critical Habitat Unit. The land is considered the most threatened tortoise habitat in the Western Mojave. It includes much of the land Fort Irwin occupies and desires, including Superior Valley.

The tortoise and the tank were in a standoff. In 1999, Congress intervened, asking relevant parties — the BLM, Fish and Wildlife, the U.S. Geological Survey, the California Department of Fish and Game and a variety of experts, including Dr. Kristin Berry, America's foremost tortoise researcher — to convene the Desert Tortoise Panel and come to some kind of agreement. The Army proposed the Modified Southern Alternative, which to some bore a striking, though scaled-back, resemblance to the Army's failed original plan. The panel rejected the proposal as it stood, but did come up with a $400 million plan to offset the expansion's effects. Much of the money would go toward buying up private lands to create tortoise reserves. Dr. Berry, California Fish and

Game and Ray Bransfield, the Fish and Wildlife Service's main tortoise guy, didn't even endorse the panel's improved plan, saying it provided no scientific rationale as to how it would safeguard the tortoises. After that, it seemed that only an act of God would get Fort Irwin its land.

It wasn't God; it was Congress, in the form of a rider, sponsored by Democratic senator Dianne Feinstein and the district's Republican congressman, Jerry Lewis (chair of the House Appropriations Committee and honored by *Rolling Stone* in 2006 as one of the 10 worst Congress members), attached to a larger appropriations bill at the end of 2000. In January 2002, President Bush, perhaps knowing something the rest of us didn't at the time, signed into law the Fort Irwin Military Lands Withdrawal Act of 2001. In a new political climate, Fish and Wildlife signed off on the plan in 2004. It appropriated $75 million for tortoise mitigations, mostly in the form of land acquisitions, but it included $8.5 million in research and monitoring money aimed at measuring the long-term impacts of translocation on the tortoises. It was a windfall for tortoise study, but it also meant the expansion would go forward on lands deemed too critical to tortoise survival just a decade earlier.

Flight of the Tortoises

Wagstaffe, with a healthy supply of cigarettes in tow, drives with us east on the I-15 into the desert. About halfway to Baker, we take the Rasor Road exit, and veer north several miles into the translocation area where 40 or so tortoises are being resettled over the course of several days.

We walk up into the wilderness and find Dr. William Boarman, a jolly, bearded fellow, who is shaped a bit like an upright tortoise. He's with Conservation Science Research and Consulting, one of the project's primary contractors, and is the biologist in charge of this tortoise group. His main mission is to monitor their reproduction habits, movements, habitat choices and long-term survival rates. Other biologists, including Dr. Berry, are studying the health, stress and disease factors of the new and resident populations.

"There are four basic things we're looking at," Boarman says. "One is called hard release. It's where you take a tortoise and just stick it under a bush. The other is called a soft release, where you take a tortoise and build a burrow and put it in the burrow — give it a home initially. Most of the animals are being moved five to 20 miles from where they lived, but we've got one group that we're moving no more than a quarter-mile from where they live. So we're comparing short-distance with long-distance translocation. And we also build pens — large five-hectare [about 12-acre] pens — to see if putting them in a pen for a few months will help keep them in the area."

The tortoises being placed here were rounded up yesterday. Upon arrival, they are weighed, measured, given a quick health checkup and released. If they have transmitters, those are checked to make sure they are functional. When we come upon a sturdy-looking male that is being hard-released under a creosote bush, the favored variety for tortoises, I ask how old he is.

"Forty or 50 is what I'd guess," Boarman says. "But he could be older. They can live to be 75 or 100. You really can't tell."

I make a joke about 70 being the new 60 with these tortoises.

"Actually, I think 30 is the new 60," says Boarman. "They are dying young now."

I ask how traumatic this type of relocation is on the animals.

"I don't know," he says, resignedly. "We can't get into his brain. I don't know what he's thinking, but what we have found most of them do, once they start moving around, is leave the area. They know it's not home and they're looking for home, I think.

"They do seem to have some sense roughly what direction home is in. Most of them are moving north."

North is Fort Irwin, where they came from. But they won't be able to get back in because one of the mitigations required that a fence be built on each side of Fort Irwin Road. The fence is 18 inches above and below ground and covers a total of 74 miles, including both sides of the road. It cost $900,000 to build.

"That fence is going to be tortoise Wounded Knee," I suggest. Everybody laughs, somewhat uncomfortably.

"It could be, and that's what we are looking at," says Boarman.

I say I'm worried about our middle-aged male right here.

"That's what this stuff is for," Wagstaffe chimes in. "We've never done this size translocation before. We'd like them to be really happy here and stay, but we don't know. You can't judge on a couple of tortoises, but when you move as many as we're moving, this is going to give us a great statistical analysis of what happens."

"We're not dumping and running," he adds. "They'll be tracking these guys for years."

But when I remind everybody that the western expansion, involving some 1,200 more tortoises, will be taking place in the next year and a half, Boarman says, "The original plan was for this to help inform that translocation. But . . . the best-laid plans of mice and men."

So, then, what is this study for?

"There is going to be so much future development in Southern California; everything is expanding. Other military bases may expand. There will be housing developments coming in. All of those have the potential of resulting in tortoise translocations, so any of those that do result in translocation can be helped by what we find out here. Also, decisions on whether or not to allow translocations. If this is a complete failure, then you would expect the translocations might not happen in the future."

I suggest that perhaps the tortoises can't afford for this to be a complete failure.

"It could be a real mess if it's a complete failure," Boarman admits.

"Apocalyptic?"

"I don't know, but it wouldn't be good. As a scientist, I wouldn't be willing to go so far as to say it would be cataclysmic for the tortoises. I just don't know because we don't have enough good population models to really evaluate so far."

The signs out here in the field today aren't promising. We inspect a man-made burrow — a soft-release attempt — in a nearby wash. The tortoise dropped there has already boogied and is nowhere to be seen.

Then, in a scene as surreal as any I've witnessed out here, a red helicopter appears over a patch of mountains, ferrying a payload of tortoises. It circles around and then lands in a flat area just above the wash where we are standing. Out of the helicopter emerge 14 tortoises, which had been watered down and kept in plastic crates overnight before their ride, as well as one biologist, Dr. Paula Kahn, charged with placing this crew, and a burly pilot straight out of central casting. It's critical to get the tortoises out of their crates and under a creosote bush or into a burrow before it gets too hot.

I decide I can't stand around and watch, and pitch in to help Dr. Kahn and the pilot release the crate-bound passengers. I swear my intentions are directed solely on the welfare of the tortoises and have nothing to do with the fact that the long-locked Dr. Kahn is a combination of brains and beauty that would be alluring even if she didn't happen to be the only person out here on this day who doesn't look like a tortoise.

As we introduce them to their new homes, each tortoise is measured, weighed, checked for signs of upper-respiratory disease and placed — rather crudely, it seems — under a creosote bush and left to its fate.

Ever the optimist, Wagstaffe opines that the tortoises must have enjoyed their helicopter ride because they don't appear to have shit or pissed themselves, which could dehydrate them and also attract predators.

I ask Dr. Kahn for her take on our friends' future here.

"They are really, really bright animals, but you have to remember, some of these tortoises — we're taking them out of a home in which they've lived for 40, 50, 60 years. It's the only thing they know and we're going to take them here and say, 'Okay, new place, different plants, everything's in a new location' . . . so it's going to take them some time."

We get the airlifted tortoises in place just before the sun reaches its peak. On the way back to the car, I spot old number 166.614 2554, the guy hightailing it for home that I mentioned before. Despite what's been done to him, he's got a strange charisma as he plods on across the wash, full of dignity and determination — or is it indignation? Up close, it's easy to believe desert tortoises are sentient beings. The ones I've seen, I'd stop to listen to if they were on a soapbox in a park. I ask Dr. Kahn if she thinks they have emotions.

"I always anthropomorphize," Dr. Kahn says. "You know, after working with them for so long, I feel on some levels they could, because they definitely have a social structure, and I know that doesn't imply emotion, but as a tortoise hugger, I'd like to think that they do have emotion. I don't know that they necessarily feel love, but they certainly feel stress, which is a physiological response . . . but I've seen tortoises gravitate towards other tortoises and, you know, they definitely have some kind of bond, or some kind of relationships. But I know that, scientifically, I can't really back that up."

The big male pauses, as if he's considering what we're saying.

"He's a ham and an old guy," says Kahn. "I bet he gets all the girls."

"Will he be all right?" I ask.

"Yeah, I think he'll be all right."

The Tortoise in You

Ileene Anderson isn't so sure. Anderson is a diminutive blonde, a biologist with a kind face who looks ready to go for a hike at a moment's notice. She's with the Center for Biological Diversity, a litigious conservation group that's been successful in defending species rights by bringing the full force of the Endangered Species Act to bear. When we meet at a loud and grungy coffee shop in Hollywood, the closest thing to nature is nearby Runyon Canyon, known more for the fragrant aroma of dog shit than desert tortoises. Nonetheless, the fate of the tortoises has been part of the center's and Anderson's life for many years. The center was part of the coalition that turned back Fort Irwin's expansion plans around the turn of the century. Now, the Army is expanding the base into the very areas most experts once thought removing tortoises from would be a bad idea.

Despite the Army's congressional mandate to do so, Anderson says, some modest sleight of hand was still required to justify the expansion. "The reason they didn't get a jeopardy biological opinion on essentially the same piece of land they'd gotten a jeopardy opinion on 10 years ago was because Fish and Wildlife Services evaluated the impact of that acreage based on the *whole* Mojave Desert population of desert tortoise and, of course, found that it wouldn't kill all the tortoises," says Anderson. "The environmental community was shocked and dismayed."

And not just because common sense tells you it might not be the best idea to remove an animal population from a habitat where it has thrived and put it in another it is unfamiliar with. Besides that, Anderson says, not enough studies have been conducted to determine if the new site can host such a significant influx. There is also the threat of predation, human encroachment, development and, most troubling, the mixing of healthy translocated tortoises with a resident population that is suffering to some degree from contagious upper-respiratory-tract disease.

What a difference eight years, a couple of wars, an act of Congress and $75 million can make. Now, many environmentalists who previously opposed the effort are dining off the government cheese brought to the table by the tortoises.

"It is my opinion that when word got out that Fort Irwin had $75 million to spend on the tortoise, it was a gold rush," says Anderson.

Or, as Michael Connor, California director of the Western Watersheds Project, a conservation group that opposes the translocation, put it when I spoke to him by phone, "Almost all of the desert-tortoise biologists are working for the government, and their job is to get the job done."

To add to the ironies, Connor says the Army's epic tortoise translocation is now the de facto funding source for the Bureau of Land Management's long-in-the-making Desert Tortoise Recovery Plan. "The money became a linchpin to sort of finance the West Mojave Plan, which should have been financed anyway," he tells me.

Of course, uprooting a rare, thriving population and moving it to a lesser habitat wasn't part of the plan. It's just part of the *Brazil*-like absurdity inherent in that parallel universe out at Fort Irwin, where fake palm trees blow over in fake Iraqi towns with fake imams and fake mosque bells. Where the Army drops $57 million to build the largest urban training center in the world, and stones are flown in from Iraq to create our own American Fallujah. And where $75 million to remove some tortoises from the fringes of the Army's land is just the cost of doing business.

"I think they just saw an opportunity to expand their fiefdom," says Anderson, "and, frankly, we're seeing exactly the same thing happen with the Marine base out in Twentynine Palms. They are wanting to expand as well."

If Fort Irwin manages to expand to the west as well, as seems likely, it will have China Lake Naval Weapons Center, often rumored to be facing retirement, flanking its south and west borders. "So," Anderson says, "the notion always was that if Fort Irwin could surround it on two sides by expanding, they would probably be able to pick up that area for subsequent use."

It's quite a success story for a base that was all but on its ass in the not-too-distant past. It's something less for the California desert tortoise, which has been in this desert pasture for a million years but is now under siege.

The fight isn't completely over. On July 2, the Center for Biological Diversity filed a federal lawsuit against the Army and the Bureau of Land Management over Fort Irwin's expansion and translocation of tortoises, the first stage of which the center has called "disastrous."

In its announcement, the center says, "Though we can't stop the Fort's expansion, we can ensure that the relocation of these rare animals is done right. With the severity of the impacts to the tortoise from the expansion, it's imperative that the Army's mitigation be as successful as possible . . . This spring's relocated tortoises suffered devastating initial mortality from predators: Within days more than 20 tortoises had been killed by coyotes. Healthy tortoises were also moved into areas where diseased tortoises live, which is in direct conflict with the recommendations of epidemiologists. The lands into which the tortoises were moved are far poorer habitat because of numerous roads, illegal off-road vehicle routes, houses, illegal dumping and mines. (This is why the area currently supports a low number of existing desert tortoise, some of which are diseased.) Subsequent phases of the relocation effort will involve over 1,000 tortoises, although relocation sites have yet to be identified."

The center says the relocation efforts could be improved by reducing the number of tortoises being moved, ensuring only healthy tortoises are moved into healthy populations, providing predator protection and improving the habitat quality of relocation areas by making them tortoise preserves.

Meanwhile, I wonder if old number 166.614.2554 has found his home.

MUTT AND JOE

First published in the LA Weekly

A beautiful day in the neighborhood begins with a cup of coffee and my dog, Max. Together we indulge in an early-morning stroll along the root-mangled sidewalks of Bronson Canyon. He sniffs. I sip. I wonder what happened to my youth; he wonders where his teeth went. I size up single-family homes with backyards; he sizes up more toothsome dogs with bouncy legs. We both glare at speeding cars.

Max often mistakes baby carriages and trash cans for past rivals or impending challengers. His hackles rise and he assumes the position. I often mistake people's words and actions for their character and intentions. My blood rushes, and I seek contrition. These are the dumb ways of dumber days. We are both trying to do that less, the better to conserve our energy for when it's really needed. I tell him to piss on a tree instead. He makes me notice the trees. We're training for middle age like two tentative skinny-dippers, toeing the water until our fear passes. Where will we go from here?

Wherever it is, Max will ensure that we'll always stop to smell the roses. And the poppies, and the sunflowers, and the ivy, and the lemon trees, and the cacti, not to mention the dog poop some irresponsible human left cooking on the sidewalk. His nose knows no boundaries. It's an equal-opportunity sniffer. It leads him, and he leads me — up from our rugged concrete to the white gray trunk of oleander and its exploding fuchsia-colored flowers, over to the violet blooms of jacaranda rubbing elbows with the ripe oranges dangling from a tree that is framed on a blue-sky background interrupted by the jutting white beams of a craftsman cottage and the green leaves of a towering oak.

Sometimes on our morning walk Max will lead me to a parked car in which someone is sprawled asleep in the back seat. Or slurping coffee while scanning a newspaper before the job starts. I know why they've picked this place to chill, and I'm glad that no matter how hard it tries, Los Angeles can't always pave over or price out the respite its natural bounty offers.

Max found me about a year ago at the farmers' market in Hollywood. I think he liked my scars and scrapes, skinny legs, black top and tawny belly. Maybe he saw something familiar in my craggy countenance and its suggestion of hereditary struggles. Whatever it was, we've been prowling this neighborhood together ever since.

I don't necessarily pine for Max and the canyon while I'm at my tiny, claustrophobic office in a converted motel on a skanky section of Hollywood Boulevard, trying to wring paying prose out of dead air and floppy sweat. But I do look forward to the finish of the summer workday, when we head for the slice of Griffith Park at the end of our street. Here, a fairly wild section of Mount Hollywood rises from the residential zoning like an enchanted forest at the end of the road. Max and I like to hike there in the low sun.

During these excursions, Max gets his woof on by chasing after other dogs. Occasionally he manages to find some four-legged community in a meadow-cum–dog park near the base of the trail. I get my call-of-the-wild fix. Here in the middle of America's most development-friendly city, I've seen rattlesnakes, tarantulas, owls, hawks, jackrabbits, road runners, coyotes and, in the rainy season, the rarest of all sights — wild, running water cascading through rocky canyon drainages. At the top of Mount

Hollywood (the peak to the east of the Hollywood sign), we bask in a 360-degree panorama of the basin. In the winter, snowcapped Mount Baldy looms over the San Gabriels. Look north at dusk and see the megawatt platelets of the Ventura Boulevard artery bringing life to the Valley. Out in the water, Catalina looks like an emerald isle.

***

A beautiful day in my neighborhood ends around midnight with Max and me padding back up Canyon Drive toward the park. Modest-size homes line the street in a potluck buffet of shapes and styles. As I pass, I sneak a peek through the windows to see what shenanigans are going on in the radiant glow of the electronic hearth. I am a happy voyeur stuck for now outside the gates of home ownership. But I imagine what it would be like on the inside, and for the first time, I imagine it's good. Meanwhile, Max investigates the dogs that poke their snouts through holes in the hedges. I wonder if he has yard envy.

Along our route, set back from the street a bit, is a larger property about which I had long been curious. On the lower half of the lot are a streambed, an old canoe and a guesthouse. Back away from the street and up on the hill stands an ominous main house that could be used for an establishing shot in a horror flick. One night curiosity got the best of us, and we ventured past the gate onto the property. As luck would have it, the owner was out cheerfully stalking the grounds, and didn't mind our intrusion. He told me the property had been a "hunting lodge" belonging to a big movie star from Hollywood's golden era. In fact, he said, this canyon was lined with "hunting lodges" of a special sort — which had earned Bronson Canyon the nickname "Bordello Canyon."

Frequently, I bring my skateboard. Max knows this means a race home. As we reach the end of the smooth blacktop about a mile up from Franklin Avenue, his tail wags excitedly and he begins eagerly to pace in circles. After a minute or so of pre-game bonding, I point the board downhill and push off, picking up speed on the modest decline. Max canters behind at first as I serpentine through the broken yellow lines and roll over the speed bumps under the hazy luminosity of streetlights. With a little cajoling, he pulls up alongside. I scoot down on my board and give him a hug as we cruise. He licks his approval. We're out here in the middle of the tree-lined drive under the cover of midnight, having our joke while the neighbors fall off to sleep.

Once, about halfway through this dash, a huge, shadowy form jumped out from the murk beyond the streetlights and onto the road in front of us. I was startled, but stayed on my skateboard, with Max right behind me. What the hell was it? I picked up speed as the degree of decline increased at a dark patch of road a few hundred yards north of the Bronson and Canyon intersection. I heard it scrape the top of a speed bump. Max shifted into full sprint to keep up.

We closed enough distance to grasp the regal stature and fluid grace of whatever it was we were following downhill. I was caught in a confluence of the untamed and the overly tame, trying to ride it for all it was worth.

Just then, a parked car flashed on its headlights. I've often wondered what must have been the driver's first thought upon seeing a large buck deer, with a full rack of antlers, being trailed by a 37-year-old man on a skateboard who was himself being chased by a toothless, runty German shepherd mutt — all of them whooshing down the middle of the street at half past midnight.

Did he rub his eyes and say, "Where the hell am I?"

PROPELLED ON A ZEPHYR
OF COMPRESSED WIND

First published in The Surfer's Journal

Stored somewhere deep in the permanent collection of the Smithsonian Institution's National Museum of American History, along with other markers of pre-collapse American life gleaned from hundreds of years of material history, is a singular surfboard almost as mysterious and only slightly less powerful than the lost Ark of the Covenant.

Should you somehow have occasion to peruse the tens of thousands of artifacts collecting dust deep in the Smithsonian underworld and stumble upon this surfboard, you might not even look twice. It is unremarkable on its face: a mid-'60s longboard with a clean deck, from a time when most surfboards were intentionally unassuming. Or, as Skip Engblom says of that era's sticks: "Big or short, they just look like they look."

And, at first glance, so would this one. If, however, you were able to flip it over for a bottoms-up view, the paradigm shift this surfboard represents would start to reveal itself in layers, as would the trail of the man responsible for it: Craig Stecyk.

The board we speak of is a stringer-less 9'5" made by Dave Sweet, circa 1966. Sweet, one of the most influential shapers of his era, was part of the polymath postwar Ocean Park, Santa Monica, neighborhood in which Stecyk came of age. Ocean Park was then a beachside barrio that before too long would be known as Dogtown following a separate, but entirely related, exercise in culture jamming by a more seasoned Stecyk.

It was in 1950, though, right around the time Stecyk had slipped the womb, that Sweet just barely beat Laguna Beach boys Gordon "Grubby" Clark and Hobie Alter to market with the first polyurethane foam blanks. This point of fact may not be 100 percent settled, but, regardless, the lighter blanks made for more-responsive boards and ushered in what we can get away with calling the modern age of performance-based surfing.

By 1966, Stecyk was a teenager spending considerable time in Sweet's shop. This was due to a variety of propinquities, not the least of which was the affinity for hotrods and custom-car culture running through the Sweet and Stecyk family trees. The July 1963 issue of *Car Craft* magazine — the "Wild 'Woodies' and Surf Wagons!" issue — serves as an apt marker of these culture confluences. On the cover, you'll see the lovely Bonnie Sweet in a baby-blue bikini, pretending to pull a single-fin log off the top of what appears to be a classic, customized 1932 Ford wagon.

At that same time, Stecyk's father was in cahoots with the brothers Sam and George Barris, and young Craig would frequently park it around the seminal Barris Kustom Shop in Lynwood, where he watched Kenny "Von Dutch" Howard hand-letter custom finishes and absorbed, literally and figuratively, different varieties of paint formulation and application techniques.

As for the '66 Sweet Smithsonian board, and other, more recognizable sticks Stecyk was messing with at the time, we can see the artist starting to hone a signature move: Take the opportunity presented by a technological breakthrough — synthetic blanks, in this case — follow the cues of custom culture and turn performance into something performative. Stecyk realized these new blanks were ripe for content and commentary, and, consciously or not, he set about postmodernizing the soft-hued suburban-escapist patina right the hell out of them.

Years later, he and his familiar accomplices would — more notoriously and more self-consciously — do the same when polyurethane wheels accelerated a performance paradigm shift in skateboarding. In this context, we can think of the Smithsonian board as totemic of the explosive impact Stecyk would have on arguably two of the biggest cultural influences since the Beatles landed at Kennedy Airport: surf and skate. Museum, meet meta. Meta, meet museum.

***

Of course, the Smithsonian wasn't entirely aware of what it was getting. By the time it took possession of Stecyk's board, that board was already a relic from the artist's past, one that landed in the Smithsonian's permanent collection as part of a massive retrospective called *A Material World*. The exhibition ran at the Institution's National Museum of American History from April 8, 1988, to December 1, 2002.

The show was intended to be a survey of how hundreds of years of technological advances have impacted the materials we use to make stuff. In a 1991 review, the *Journal of American History* put it this way: "The exhibition aims to increase the museum visitor's awareness of the importance of the materials that compose goods, to show how the choice of materials both affects the function of the goods and reveals or reflects broader cultural values, and to demonstrate how the materials used for goods in the same function changed or were replaced by other, often newer, materials."

The objects on display spanned nearly 300 years of American history (from a primarily non-indigenous perspective) and ran the gamut from pre-industrial millstones and whale-oil lamps to early industrial home technologies like sewing machines and metal-fused household items. Things start to get real Kandy-Kolored Tangerine-Flake Streamline Baby–ish (to cop from the

Barris-inspired eponymous essay in Tom Wolfe's first collection) when the "American" century kicks into high gear, starting with the Art Deco era and hitting hyper speed during the postwar boom.

And because there was, as Mr. McGuire said to Benjamin Braddock out by the pool in *The Graduate*, "a great future in plastics," and because history was just a year from being over in 1988 (and surely done by the time *A Material World* rolled up its runners), Stecyk's surfboard landed in the show's "Synthetic Realms" section, an unwitting icon of new composites and disruptive art. There, *The New York Times* noted in a contemporaneous review, it stood alongside such items as a chrome-plated toaster, an Electrolux vacuum cleaner, artificial hearts, a vintage *American Graffiti*–style jukebox, electric toothbrushes and, I read somewhere, Dragsters.

Current context may have rendered these objects sentimental signifiers of more innocent times, but as Robert Post, the exhibition's curator, told the *Times*, "Materials have to affect human values. 'Plastic' means infinitely moldable. When people can define what they want and fire up a plan, they feel in charge of their environment, but people also lose power over nature as certain craft skills are lost."

People can also lose the script at the confluence of art, lifestyle and commerce, even in the postmodern commodification complex, also known as branding, that Stecyk would help erect during his Zephyr and Powell-Peralta iterations, but was only starting to mess with back in 1966. So, it's probably not a coincidence that he was already showing an astute awareness of what he had helped to be wrought, willingly or not, by the time the Smithsonian's gears were grinding away on *A Material World*.

In fact, as the behemoth Smithsonian exhibition was getting ready to open its doors, a then-38-year-old Stecyk and Laguna Art Museum director Charles Desmarais were putting the finishing touches on the artist's sly investigation of those very issues. *Papa Moana*, for which Bolton Colburn's companion catalog is a must-read for attempting to grasp Stecyk's nearly unfathomable impact on our culture, cheekily debuted in 1989 at South Coast Plaza, the mall serving as a museum satellite.

If brevity is the soul of wit, I dare say *Papa Moana* made the more powerful statement about the dizzying impact of materials and manifest destiny (and plastics!) during the postwar boom that was pretty much out of steam by the time Reagan limped off into the sunset.

***

Like I said, though, you'd have to turn that Smithsonian board over to notice anything out of the ordinary.

"The deck was clear. It was at times collaged / air brushed/ painted on in this area. It was ironically returned to its unadorned state, since the Smithsonian show theme was [*A*] *Material World*, about the impact of technology on recreational activities," Stecyk explains. "The Smithsonian asked for it for its appropriateness for their overall exhibition premise. It was displayed in close proximity to Charles and Ray Eames fiberglass chairs."

The flip side is where things got weird.

Stecyk had been tinkering with offset fins for enhanced performance (he might have tried clipping a couple feet), and the offset made the bottom appear asymmetrical. There, he had his way with it. "The bottom of the board is a five-colored abstract resin job that I executed. It was an experimental personal board and not standard issue," says Stecyk, who describes its overall impression as "uncontrolled abstract — something between a Jackson Pollock and a toy marble. It had depths and layers and streaks."

I have to take his word for it because I haven't seen it. Few have, and nobody seems to be able to find an image of the permanent-collection board itself, although I have independently confirmed it exists and was indeed permanently collected.

Even Stecyk lost track of the board for a while. As the story goes, it went missing sometime after he had stashed it in a commandeered storage space beneath the Pacific Ocean Park Pier. In those days, Stecyk was a raft wrangler for Kent Sherwood, Jay Adams' stepfather, who had the Ely's Beach Rentals concession stand. The board would likely have gone down with the POP ship, which by then was taking on the financial water that would soon tank it like the Atlantis of amusement parks, had it not turned up like a bad penny in a storage space Nathan Pratt kept under the pier.

Pratt apparently brought the board out of storage as a prop for a Horizons West (erstwhile Zephyr shop) photo shoot for *GQ* magazine. Stecyk happened by when the board washed ashore. He reclaimed it from obscurity and eventually shipped it off to the Smithsonian for posterity.

Maybe it's better left the stuff of legend, for it may not be the best representation of what Stecyk was up to at that time. By 1966, he was already well into fucking with the Miki Dora boards coming out of Greg Noll's shop.

"I painted a lot of boards for an assortment of individuals," Stecyk says. "A number of things were done with Dora, and I received Cat project boards directly from Greg Noll [whose boards Dora was then riding]. Tak Kawahara was my shaper of choice in Greg's stable. Da Bull's joy over my art desecration of his efforts, and the messes I left behind in what was then the 'world's biggest modern surfboard manufacturing facility' are the basis of our decades-long friendship."

***

I have seen one example of Stecyk's Dora boards from that time, and it's quite arresting. Painted on its deck is a crude, nose-to-tail tarantula (the 16-year-old Stecyk was into them) with the Greg Noll and Da Cat logos caught in a web within the thorax. The mixed-media image was rendered with brush paint, sprayed automotive lacquer, decoupage, ink drawing and hand aerosol applications.

That might help explain the process, but the sheer transgression of the art, done for that era's most transgressive surfer, is hard to overstate. Stecyk, of course, will do his best to understate it.

"It has overt painting and doesn't have seagulls and all that hippie crap," he says. "It's much closer to a graffiti practice."

That it would be so is not surprising given that Stecyk's free-range adolescence involved navigating between two different gang territories, making it incumbent to learn to decode the graffiti messages. Stecyk was also presciently attuned to the growing impact of Chicano art and culture on the larger landscape. The Mexican muralist David Alfaro Siqueiros, whose 1932 *America Tropical* on the south facade of Italian Hall in El Pueblo kicked off the mural era in L.A., was a significant influence.

"I continue to be an associate of Siqueiros' grandson," says Stecyk. LACMA's 1974 exhibit of the famed Los Four Chicano art collective would be similarly influential.

Not that Stecyk had to go looking for influences. He was born into them.

"Growing up around the Barris brothers' car customization shop, seeing Von Dutch hand-lettering there and visiting the Ford assembly plant where my father was employed meant that I was exposed to a variety of paint formulation and application techniques. The commercial-split, fountain-color technique used by commercial printers was another influence," he says. "My father used Sharpe spray guns in his pursuits of auto restyling and furniture building. My mother, in the glazing of her ceramic pieces, utilized that same equipment. Periodically we would venture to Sharpe's manufacturing headquarters in downtown Los Angeles to pick up replacement parts. I subsequently employed

Sharpe spray equipment in the painting of surf and skateboards, as well as posters, bikes, etc."

As for how and when he started viewing surfboard decks as canvases, Stecyk says, "Surf vehicles are graphic surfaces, which optically interact with conflicting environments and situational contexts. The dynamism of the air versus the water perpetually is at crossed purposes in the vicinity of the intersection of sea and land. Skateboards were originally referred to as sidewalk surfboards. I enjoy these dichotomies and communicate this discord."

Indeed, the Dora board and others he would later spray paint under the Zephyr imprimatur can be viewed as examples of an artist finding his voice in this discord. Here is Stecyk just starting to assemble the disruption bomb of hard-edged West Coast bohemia he would soon drop into the middle of the *Gidget*-cum–*The Endless Summer* stasis that had been gripping the scene. You can look at that board and see the point at which a 16-year-old's artistic DNA started commanding the lexicon of decades' worth of youth culture and street art.

"He was the first person that I know of who would have brought spray-painting artwork to surfboards. In terms of graffiti, he's definitely the guy," says Colburn. "It was subversive, a thread to the Beautiful Losers era." As the years passed, those Dora boards became harder to find. Indeed, when Claudine Klose, who was a curator for *A Material World* and who also happened to be Miki Dora's first cousin, came calling about a surfboard for the show, Stecyk recalls that "Miki had absolutely no interest in it, which would be typical of Miki . . . Miki managed to self-limit everything."

So, off went Stecyk's Dave Sweet board. And that is the tale of how the board in the Smithsonian's permanent collection, while certainly a hallmark of postwar progress in synthetic compounds and of proto-punk sensibilities, is sort of there by default.

***

That's okay — those mid-'60s boards were just the seeds. The big bloom came almost an entire Vietnam War later, when Stecyk suggested to Skip Engblom and Jeff Ho that they put his airbrushing techniques into production at the Zephyr shop.

"Jeff and I looked at him like, 'How are you going to do that?'" recalls Engblom.

To answer, Stecyk came in one day and started hooking up an airbrush. It may have been the very same vintage Sharpe Model 25 Stecyk's mother had been using for her ceramics practice. They experimented with paints and tapes and colors and techniques. "It wasn't like we did it one day and bing, it worked," says Engblom.

After a series of misfires, mostly with the resin rejecting the paint during the glassing phase, Stecyk suggested lacquer. They did the paint job. They glassed. The resin and paint held. Soon they discovered they could use lacquer-based spray cans and, with the right tape, at last hold a sharp line.

At the same time, they were trying to add something more to the sharp lines and flat graphics, something deeper. "We were trying to do multidimensional, layered colors. It was a continuing process of trying to get more depth, more depth," Engblom explains. "Craig was laying down undercoats and coming back and frosting other coats over it — with lacquer right out of the can."

Once they got the techniques dialed in, they didn't look back.

"We were a full year or 18 months ahead of Rainbow. We had to keep the fucking doors open. We had a product that no one else had. It was cooler. It was way cooler," says Engblom. "A lot of people really liked what we did, and a lot of people really hated it. For better or worse, we were the problem or the solution."

AUTHOR'S NOTE

More than two decades ago, something wonderful happened. Iris Berry's address in the map of my life changed from someone I knew of (who didn't?), to someone I knew. And now, this book is here because of the more than two decades of friendship, inspiration and encouragement that small but significant move has afforded me. What a gift. Thank you, Iris.

It's also here because of a larger change in address, the one that brought me out here when I was too old to be a young man, but too young to know it yet. That, too, has been a gift. For, my SoCal days have been rife with the sorts of friends, colleagues and just plain interesting people who have enriched my life and, in some cases, filled these pages. I'm grateful to all of you.

For his generous foreword, a big hug to Jamie Brisick, whose talent and growth keeps defying gravity.

For her love, patience and partnership, a big kiss to my wife, Ingrid.

As for what we have here . . . well, there's no transactional reason for this book to exist. It's not going to make anybody any money and most of the pieces in it are already floating, like cosmic dust, around the ever-expanding digital universe.

So, what's the point?

Maybe, when you put them together in one place, some kind of form takes shape. Maybe all these fragments, the lives and stories and geographies that were once bound ineffably together, and are now, thanks to Punk Hostage Press, tangibly so, add up to something. Maybe a hazy portrait of a time and a place comes into view. Maybe there's some kind of ragged history here. Anyway, that's what Iris said, and she made me believe her.

Maybe you will, too.

Joe Donnelly – 2022

PUBLISHER'S NOTE

Getting to work with an author on their book is a big, beautiful deal, an important and honorable task. If you would have told me when we started Punk Hostage Press in 2012 that we would one day publish Joe Donnelly, I wouldn't have believed you. Joe Donnelly is the writer's writer. The raconteur's raconteur. He has supported and celebrated me and so many other writers along the way. He has kept me inspired and made me believe that what I do has purpose. But that's Joe. He sees and writes with his heart. And he writes phenomenally. Joe's love for Southern California and its denizens pens itself elegantly from his compassion for the human condition and his deep appreciation for an ever-changing West Coast aesthetic that Joe himself has helped shape. Publishing this book is a real honor. Thank you, Joe.

Iris Berry
Punk Hostage Press
February 2, 2022

MORE ABOUT THE BOOK

In *Kill Bill 2*, the bride asked the pimp, Where is Bill? Where is Bill? Why start this way? Well first off, it's fun and, second, I have you this far down the line. Joe is not a pimp. He is, in fact, 180 degrees away from one. I have known him for a number of years now and I have to say he will give an honest account of things and stories told to him and he will dig in and call bullshit on bullshit and that's all you can ask for these days. Like they say in the movies, just facts, Jack.

—**Skip Engblom**, Dogtown and Z-boys legend, artist, impresario

In place, character, and experience, Donnelly's latest collection is sharp in observation and dripping in bona fides. Blessed with the skill set of decades working in hard-nosed journalism, as well as the when-where-who discerning eye of someone comfortable on the fringes, each and every story lets loose the controls and leads you down backroads, both literal and figurative, you'd never sniff out otherwise. *So Cal* and its author are definitive of a region that rails against definition — even as he drags the reader up and down and out and away and back again.

—**Whitman Bedwell**, editor in chief, *The Surfer's Journal*

When I think about writers and editors who've inspired me, Joe Donnelly is at the top of the list. Not only on a personal level as someone who has been lucky enough to work with and learn from him, but as a reader who admires engaging, beyond-the-basics journalism. Joe's always-vivid approach to storytelling conveys unique insight and an intimacy that anyone can connect with, no matter the subject.

—**Lina Lecaro**, journalist, *LA Weekly* editor

MORE ABOUT THE AUTHOR

Joe Donnelly is a journalist and writer living in Southern California. He teaches English and journalism at Whittier College. His previous collection, *L.A. Man: Profiles from a Big City and a Small World*, was published by Rare Bird Books. Donnelly has earned numerous recognitions for his journalism. His short story "Bonus Baby" was selected for the 2016 O. Henry Prize Collection, and "50 Minutes," written with Harry Shannon, was selected for *The Best American Mystery Stories*.

MORE BOOKS ON PUNK HOSTAGE PRESS

Danny Baker
    Fractured - 2012
A Razor
    Better Than a Gun in A Knife Fight - 2012
    Drawn Blood: Collected Works
    From D.B.P.LTD., 1985-1995 - 2012
    Beaten Up Beaten Down – 2012
    Small Catastrophes in A Big World - 2012
    Half- Century Status – 2013
    Days of Xmas Poems - 2014
    Puro Purismo - 2021
Iris Berry
    The Daughters of Bastards – 2012
    All That Shines Under the Hollywood Sign – 2019
    The Trouble with Palm Trees – 2021
    Gas Station Etiquette - 2022
C.V. Auchterlonie
    Impress - 2012
Yvonne De la Vega
    Tomorrow, Yvonne - Poetry & Prose for Suicidal Egoists - 2012
Carolyn Srygley- Moore
    Miracles Of the Blog: A Series - 2012
Rich Ferguson
    8th & Agony -2012
Jack Grisham
    Untamed -2013
    Code Blue: A Love Story ~ 2014
    Pulse of the World. Arthur Chance, Punk Rock Detective - 2021
Dennis Cruz
    Moth Wing Tea - 2013
    The Beast Is We - 2018
Frank Reardon
    Blood Music - 2013
Pleasant Gehman
    Showgirl Confidential – 2013
    Rock 'n' Roll Witch – A Memoir of Sex Magick, Drugs and Rock 'n' Roll
    – 2022
Hollie Hardy
    How To Take a Bullet and Other Survival Poems – 2022
SB Stokes
    History Of Broken Love Things – 2014

MORE BOOKS ON PUNK HOSTAGE PRESS

A.D. Winans
>   *Dead Lions* – 2014

Joel Landmine
>   *Yeah, Well...* – 2014
>   *Things Change* - 2021

Michele McDannold
>   *Stealing The Midnight from A Handful of Days* – 2014
>   SpaceTime Continuum for Dummies - 2021

S.A. Griffin
>   *Dreams Gone Mad with Hope* - 2014

Nadia Bruce- Rawlings
>   *Scars* - 2014
>   *Driving in The Rain* - 2020

Lee Quarnstrom
>   *WHEN I WAS A DYNAMITER, Or, how a Nice Catholic Boy Became a Merry Prankster, a Pornographer, and a Bridegroom Seven Times* - 2014

Alexandra Naughton
>   *I Will Always Be Your Whore/Love Songs for Billy Corgan* - 2014
>   *You Could Never Objectify Me More Than I've Already Objectified Myself* -2015

Maisha Z Johnson
>   *No Parachutes to Carry Me Home* - 2015

Michael Marcus
>   *#1 Son and Other Stories* - 2017

Danny Garcia
>   *LOOKING FOR JOHNNY, The Legend of Johnny Thunders* - 2018

William S. Hayes
>   *Burden of Concrete* - 2020
>   *King of the Road* - 2022

Todd Moore
>   *Dillinger's Thompson* - 2020

Dan Denton
>   *$100-A-Week Motel* - 2021

Jack Henry
>   *Driving W/ Crazy, living with madness* – 2021

Patrick O'Neil
>   *Anarchy at The Circle K – On the Road With* Dead Kennedys, T.S.O.L., Flipper, Subhumans… and Heroin – 2022

Made in the USA
Middletown, DE
09 March 2022

62380564R00125